Cambridge Elements ≡

Elements in Phonetics
edited by
David Deterding
Universiti Brunei Darussalam

THE PHONETICS OF MALAY

David Deterding
Universiti Brunei Darussalam

Ishamina Athirah Gardiner
Universiti Brunei Darussalam

Najib Noorashid
Universiti Brunei Darussalam

CAMBRIDGE
UNIVERSITY PRESS

University Printing House, Cambridge CB2 8BS, United Kingdom

One Liberty Plaza, 20th Floor, New York, NY 10006, USA

477 Williamstown Road, Port Melbourne, VIC 3207, Australia

314–321, 3rd Floor, Plot 3, Splendor Forum, Jasola District Centre,
New Delhi – 110025, India

103 Penang Road, #05–06/07, Visioncrest Commercial, Singapore 238467

Cambridge University Press is part of the University of Cambridge.

It furthers the University's mission by disseminating knowledge in the pursuit of
education, learning, and research at the highest international levels of excellence.

www.cambridge.org
Information on this title: www.cambridge.org/9781108931922
DOI: 10.1017/9781108942836

First published 2022

A catalogue record for this publication is available from the British Library.

ISBN 978-1-108-93192-2 Paperback
ISSN 2634-1689 (online)
ISSN 2634-1670 (print)

Cambridge University Press has no responsibility for the persistence or accuracy of
URLs for external or third-party internet websites referred to in this publication
and does not guarantee that any content on such websites is, or will remain,
accurate or appropriate.

The Phonetics of Malay

Elements in Phonetics

DOI: 10.1017/9781108942836
First published online: February 2022

David Deterding
Universiti Brunei Darussalam

Ishamina Athirah Gardiner
Universiti Brunei Darussalam

Najib Noorashid
Universiti Brunei Darussalam

Author for correspondence: David Deterding, dhdeter@gmail.com

Abstract: Malay is one of the major languages in the world, but there has been relatively little detailed research on its phonetics. This Element provides an overview of existing descriptions of the pronunciation of Standard Malay before briefly considering the pronunciation of some dialects of Malay. It then introduces materials that may be used for studying the phonetics of Malay: a short text, the North Wind and the Sun (NWS) passage; and a map task, to generate conversational data. Based on recordings using these materials by two female and two male consultants who are academics at Universiti Brunei Darussalam, the Element next offers an acoustic analysis of the consonants and vowels of Malay, the syllable structure arising from fast speech processes, as well as the rhythm and intonation of the Standard Malay that is spoken in Brunei. Finally, it suggests directions for further research on the phonetics of Malay.

Audio files referenced in this title can be found at the following webpage: www.cambridge.org/phonetics-of-malay

Keywords: Malay, vowels, consonants, rhythm, intonation

ISBNs: 9781108931922 (PB), 9781108942836 (OC)
ISSNs: 2634-1689 (online), 2634-1670 (print)

Contents

1 Introduction

Malay is a member of the Malayic subgroup of Austronesian, a language family which, it has been suggested, may have originated in Taiwan between 4000 and 3000 BCE before spreading to Sumatra and the Malay Peninsula between 1500 and 500 BCE (Andaya, 2001). The Malayic subgroup includes languages like Gayo in Sumatra (Eades & Hajek, 2006), Minangkabau in Sumatra, and Iban in Borneo, as well as many local dialects of Malay spoken in Peninsular Malaysia, Borneo, Sumatra, and much of the rest of Indonesia (Adelaar, 2005).

Closely related varieties of Malay have national language status in Malaysia, Brunei Darussalam (henceforth Brunei), and Singapore, where it is called *Bahasa Melayu* ('the Malay language') (Clynes & Deterding, 2011), and in Indonesia, where it is termed *Bahasa Indonesia* (Soderberg & Olson, 2008). Some of the places where Malay is spoken are shown in Figure 1.

There is a high degree of mutual intelligibility between all these standard varieties, which are said to derive from the Malay of Johor in Peninsular Malaysia (Steinhauer, 2005), though the level of intelligibility is probably higher between varieties of the language in Malaysia, Singapore, and Brunei than with Bahasa Indonesia, partly because the lexicon of the latter has historically been substantially influenced by Dutch. Here, we will describe the pronunciation of Standard Malay, with the data for the acoustic analysis in Section 5 derived from the *baku* ('standard') variety that is promoted in Brunei and is spoken in formal situations by well-educated people there; but we acknowledge that, in reality, Standard Malay represents a range of varieties, with considerable differences in their pronunciation, and the analysis provided here cannot cover all the variation that exists in the varieties of Standard Malay spoken in Malaysia, Brunei, Singapore, and Indonesia. Further research should investigate in more depth how the pronunciation of these varieties differs.

After considering the status of Standard Malay, in Section 2 we review the existing research on its consonants, vowels, syllable structure, stress, rhythm, and intonation, and then in Section 3 we briefly consider some of the ways in which the pronunciation of other dialects of Malay differs from that of Standard Malay, though it is beyond the scope of this short overview to analyse all varieties or to assess why the differences between them occur. A more thorough coverage of phonological diversity in the Malay dialects can be found in Asmah (1991). In Section 4, we introduce some materials for obtaining spoken data for Malay, and then in Section 5 we provide an acoustic analysis of the pronunciation of the Standard Malay spoken in Brunei based on the recordings of two female and two male consultants who live in the country and are highly

Phonetics

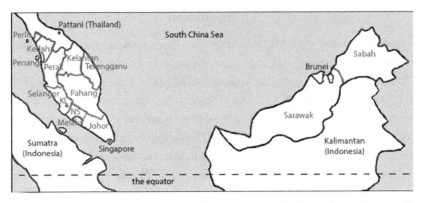

Figure 1 Map showing some of the places where Malay is spoken. KL = Kuala
Lumpur (the capital of Malaysia); NS = Negeri Sembilan.

proficient in speaking the language. Finally, in Section 6 we offer suggestions
for areas of future research on the phonetics of Malay.

1.1 Standard Malay

Some languages depend on an official organization to stipulate what is standard.
So, for example, the Académie Française decides on the pronunciation of
standard French. In contrast, other languages are more democratic, allowing
standards to emerge, so lexicographers aim to reflect current usage rather than
specify what is correct, and English is like this. For example, for the pronunciation of English, the *Longman Pronunciation Dictionary* is an authoritative
resource that includes charts and statistics on the preferences of a large number
of respondents to questionnaires; so for instance it reports that, in Britain, 55%
of people pronounce *ate* as /et/ while 45% prefer /eɪt/, with neither constituting
the single correct pronunciation, and instead they represent alternatives (Wells,
2008, p. 54).

Malay follows the French model, not that of English. In Malaysia, one of the
roles of the Dewan Bahasa dan Pustaka (DBP, 'the Language and Literature
Bureau') is to determine what is correct, and in Brunei there is a similar
organization, the Dewan Bahasa dan Pustaka Brunei (DBPB). Furthermore,
there is a cross-national organization MABBIM (*Majlis Bahasa Brunei
Indonesia Malaysia*, 'Language Council of Brunei, Indonesia and Malaysia'),
which was set up in November 1985 (Asmah, 2008, p. 73) and whose role is to
try to derive a common standard for Malay in the region, though it has never
considered pronunciation. MABBIM has focused on spelling and also deriving
common technical terms, and it has achieved success in some areas; so, for

example, it has managed to achieve a common system of spelling for Malay and Indonesian (Asmah, 1967).

Let us consider how the top-down specification of standards affects one word: *erat* ('closely'). Most speakers pronounce it as /erat/, with /e/ (a front vowel, known in Malay as *e taling*) in the first syllable, and indeed, three out of four of our consultants pronounce it this way. However, the DBP insists that the correct pronunciation is /ərat/, with /ə/ (a central vowel, termed *e pepet*) (DBP, 2013), so this is stipulated to be the standard pronunciation even if few people actually use it.

Despite the efforts of the DBP and also MABBIM to establish a common standard, there continues to be considerable variation in Standard Malay. Indeed, Asmah (1971) states that there is no uniform standard variety of Malay. Indonesian is the most divergent variety in its lexis, partly due to the influence of languages such as Dutch and Javanese, while phonetically and phonologically there is also substantial variation in the Standard Malay spoken in Peninsular Malaysia (Clynes & Deterding, 2011). The Standard Malay spoken in Brunei seems to be in an intermediate position, in many ways similar to Indonesian in its pronunciation and grammar, but more like Peninsular varieties in its lexis (Poedjosoedarmo, 1996).

In Malaysia, there are basically two standard varieties, which can be termed the 'a-variety' and the 'schwa-variety' (Asmah, 1991, p. 23). They differ primarily in the realization of two features affecting the end of a word: in the a-variety, word-final orthographic <a> is pronounced as /a/ and also word-final orthographic <r> is retained, while in the schwa-variety, word-final <a> is usually pronounced as /ə/ and word-final <r> is omitted (Asmah, 1991, p. 2).

Here we describe the a-variety of Standard Malay that is promoted in Brunei. The a-variety is also spoken in the East Malaysian states of Sarawak and Sabah, and the northern Malay states of Kedah, Perlis, and Penang. Indonesian is also an a-variety. This differs from the schwa-variety that predominates in Peninsular Malaysian places such as Kuala Lumpur (KL), Johor, Melaka, and Perak, and also in Singapore (Asmah, 1991, p. 3). Yunus (1980) describes the schwa-variety; so, for example, he gives the pronunciation of *bila* ('when') as /bilə/ (p. 17), and he notes that *pasar* ('market') is generally pronounced as /pasa/ (p. 18). He further notes (p. 73), 'Many speakers, perhaps the majority of speakers in Malaya and Singapore, do not use [r] in word final position.' Teoh (1994) also describes the schwa-variety, focusing on his own dialect spoken in Johor. However, here we primarily focus on an a-variety of Standard Malay in which final <a> is /a/ in words such as *bila* /bila/, and /r/ is pronounced at the end of words such as *pasar* /pasar/.

2 Existing Research

This section will consider existing accounts of the consonants, vowels, syllable structure, stress, rhythm, and intonation of Malay. Each of these areas will be considered in more detail in Section 5, based on recordings of four consultants reading a short passage and also engaging in brief conversational interactions.

2.1 Consonants

Table 1 shows the consonants of Standard Malay. The inventory of 24 consonants included in Table 1 is the same as that listed in Clynes and Deterding (2011). The glottal stop /ʔ/ is shown in brackets, as its inclusion might be questioned (a topic to be discussed further in Section 2.1.3). The fricatives /f, v, z, ʃ, x/ are also in brackets, as they only occur in loan words, so they have marginal status in Malay. For Indonesian, Soderberg and Olson (2008) list the same 18 basic consonants but include only four marginal consonants, omitting /v/ and /x/, though the researchers note that their speaker actually pronounced *ahkirnya* ('finally') as [axiɳa], which raises questions about the exclusion of /x/.

2.1.1 Plosives

The plosives /p, b/, /t, d/, and /k, g/ are voiceless/voiced pairs. In many varieties of Malay, /t/ is dental rather than alveolar, though not all speakers have a difference in place of articulation for /t/ and /d/. For Indonesian, Soderberg and Olson (2008) note that /t/ is dental, showing it as /t̪/, while /d/ is alveolar; but Fauzi (2018, p. 16) argues that /t/ is alveolar, and he contrasts it with the equivalent sound in Arabic, which is dental (p. 19). /k/ is velar in syllable onsets, but in the coda of a syllable, it is generally realized as a glottal stop [ʔ], though Asmah (1991, p. 7) notes that it may be [k] in some

Table 1 The consonants of Malay

	Labial	Alveolar / Dental	Post-alveolar / Palatal	Velar	Glottal
Plosive / Affricate	p b	t d	ʧ ʤ	k g	(ʔ)
Fricative	(f) (v)	s (z)	(ʃ)	(x)	h
Nasal	m	n	ɲ	ŋ	
Trill / Tap		r			
Approximant	w		j		
Lateral		l			

loanwords such as *bank*. Voiceless /p/ and /t/ are always unreleased in the coda of a syllable.

In the onset of a syllable, /p, t, k/ are normally unaspirated. However, in Brunei, some speakers, particularly radio broadcasters, have aspiration on initial /k/ (Clynes & Deterding, 2011), largely due to influence from English (Poedjosoedarmo, 1996), which is widely spoken in the country (McLellan, Noor Azam, & Deterding, 2016). The degree of aspiration for the syllable-initial voiceless plosives in the pronunciation of Standard Malay spoken in Brunei will be analysed acoustically in Section 5.1.

The voiced plosives /b, d, g/ do not occur in syllable codas in the native lexis, and when they are found in the codas of loan words, they are usually replaced with their voiceless counterparts (Teoh, 1994, p. 53), so *jawab* ('to answer'), a loan from Arabic, is generally pronounced as [dʒɐwɐp˺], and *wujud* ('to exist'), also a loan from Arabic, is [wudʒʊt˺].

2.1.2 Affricates

/tʃ/ and /dʒ/ are phonetic affricates, though phonemically they pattern with the plosives. They may have a lamino-alveolar realization with a 'noisy' release (possibly influenced by English) rather than the less affricated, post-alveolar realization typical of many Indonesian speakers (Clynes & Deterding, 2011). For Indonesian, Fauzi (2018, p. 17) similarly treats /tʃ/ and /dʒ/ as plosives (though he uses the symbols [C] and [J] for them).

The two affricates occur in initial and medial position, but they occur only in final position in loanwords such as *mac* /matʃ/ ('March') and *imej* /imedʒ/ ('image') (Asmah, 1991, p. 7).

2.1.3 Glottal Stop

The glottal stop has marginal status, and it is unclear whether it should be listed as a phoneme of Malay or not. It occurs as the realization of final /k/ (see Section 2.1.1), though the fact that [k] rather than a glottal stop occurs at the end of loanwords such as *bank* (Asmah, 1991, p. 7) suggests that the realization of word-final /k/ is variable. We might also note that, prior to the adoption of the common spelling system in Malaysia and Indonesia, the word-final glottal stop was shown as <'> in both countries, which suggests that it was accorded phonemic status at the time.

In addition, the glottal stop can occur optionally at the start of morphemes with an initial vowel. Teoh (1994, p. 26) claims that a syllable onset is obligatory in Malay, so *angin* /aŋin/ is pronounced as [ʔɐŋɪn] with an initial glottal stop; but that does not necessarily mean the glottal stop is a phoneme, as the word-initial glottal stop can be inserted by rule (Teoh, 1994, p. 59).

Word-medially, the glottal stop is also found between two vowels in two different contexts: in some Arabic loanwords like *saat* [sɐʔɐt˺] ('second'), the glottal stop occurs as the realization of the Arabic voiced pharyngeal fricative /ʕ/ (Yunus, 1980, p. 59); and the glottal stop can also occur intervocalically across a morpheme boundary, for example after certain prefixes such as *di-* (the passive prefix) as in *dianggap* /diaŋgap/ ('be considered') pronounced as [diʔɐŋgɐp˺], and before the word-final *-i* locative suffix, as in *mengenai* /məŋənai/ ('about') (for which the root is *kena*) pronounced as [məŋənɐʔi].

In summary, the glottal stop can occur in four situations: as the realization of final /k/; as an optional sound before a word-initial vowel, such as in *angin* [ʔɐŋɪn]; as a break that separates two vowels in words such as *saat* [sɐʔɐt˺] derived from Arabic; and between two vowels when a prefix ends with a vowel and the root has an initial vowel, as in *dianggap* [diʔɐŋgɐp˺], or when the root ends with a vowel and a suffix has an initial vowel, as in *mengenai* [məŋənɐʔi]. In all these four situations, the glottal stop may be derived by rule, either as realization of /k/ (Farid, 1980, p. 9) or by insertion (Farid, 1980, p. 50), so it is unclear if it should be regarded as a phoneme of Malay. Teoh (1994) asserts that the status of the glottal stop is '[o]ne of the outstanding issues in Malay phonology' (p. 58), especially as 'where one expects it to be manifested it is not, and where one expects it to be absent it shows up' (p. 59). Its phonemic status, and the contexts in which it occurs, are areas that might be investigated further in future studies of Malay phonology.

2.1.4 Nasals

There are four nasals in Malay: the bilabial nasal /m/, the alveolar nasal /n/, the palatal nasal /ɲ/, and the velar nasal /ŋ/. The velar nasal /ŋ/ is always indicated by <ng> in the spelling, even when it occurs before <k> and <g> such as in *angka* /aŋka/ ('number') and *panggil* /paŋgil/ ('call'). The palatal nasal occurs whenever there is <ny> in the spelling, such as in *nyanyi* /ɲaɲi/ ('to sing'). It also occurs before /tʃ/ and /dʒ/ in words such as *ancam* /aɲtʃam/ ('threat') and *anjing* /aɲdʒiŋ/ ('dog') (Yunus, 1980, p. 77), in which case it is spelled as <n> rather than <ny>. All four nasals can occur in word-initial position, including /ɲ/ in words such as *nyawa* ('life') and /ŋ/ in words such as *ngeri* /ŋəri/ ('frightening'), and /m/, /n/, and /ŋ/ can all occur in word-final position, in words such as *macam* ('like'), *sabun* ('soap'), and *barang* ('thing'). /ɲ/ does not occur in word-final position, and it only occurs in syllable-final position before /tʃ/ and /dʒ/.

2.1.5 Fricatives

Of the fricatives, only /s/ and /h/ are primary consonants occurring in native words of Malay. Both may occur in onset and coda position: *satu* ('one') and *hari* ('day'); and *emas* ('gold') and *rumah* ('house'). In final position, /h/ is sometimes not audible, particularly with common words such as *sudah* ('already'). The realization of syllable-final /h/ will be investigated further in Section 5.2.

The remaining five fricatives, /f, v, z, ʃ, x/, are shown in parentheses in Table 1 to indicate that they are marginal. They occur only in loanwords, generally from Arabic such as *faham* ('understand'), *zakat* ('tithe'), *syarat* /ʃarat/ ('rule'), and *khidmat* /xidmat/ ('service'), or from English such as *visa* ('visa').

Yunus (1980, p. 90) suggests that /θ/ and /ð/ also occur in loanwords from Arabic, with /θ/ as the initial consonant in words such as *salji* ('snow') and the final consonant in words like *hadith* ('teachings of the Prophet Muhammad') and /ð/ at the start of words such as *daif* ('weak'), and both Teoh (1994, p. 8) and Abdullah (2005, p. 57) also list /θ/ and /ð/ as part of the inventory of Standard Malay. However, most speakers pronounce these words with /s/ and /d/ at the start instead of /θ/ and /ð/. Noor Azam Haji-Othman (personal communication) suggests that [θ] and [ð] occur only in very careful pronunciation in a religious context, and most speakers do not use these sounds. We have therefore not listed them as phonemes of Malay in Table 1.

Indirawati and Mardian (2006, p. 54) additionally list /ž/ (which is presumably /ʒ/) as a consonant of Malay, occurring at the start of words such as *zohor* ('midday prayer'), in the middle of *hadir* (sometimes spelled *hadhir*) ('to attend'), and at the end of *haid* (sometimes spelled *haidh*) ('menstruation'). All of these are Arabic loans, and the sound may occur for the Arabic ظ (a voiced velarized interdental or alveolar fricative) at the start of *zohor* and also for the Arabic ض (a voiced velarized alveolar stop) (Ryding, 2014, p. 16) in the middle of *hadir* and at the end of *haid*. Noor Azam Haji-Othman (personal communication) confirms that [ʒ] occurs only in a religious context.

2.1.6 /r/

In the Standard Malay spoken in Brunei, /r/ can be realized as a trill [r] or a tap [ɾ] (Clynes & Deterding, 2011), and in Indonesian as well it tends to be a trill or a tap (Soderberg & Olson, 2008). However, in Perlis, Kedah, and Penang in the north-west of Peninsular Malaysia, it is often a uvular fricative [ʁ] in prevocalic or intervocalic positions and a pharyngeal fricative [ʕ] in final position, while in Sarawak it tends to be a velar fricative [ɣ] (Asmah, 1991, p. 4).

As we noted in Section 1.1, /r/ does not occur in final position in the schwa-varieties of Standard Malay, and Yunus (1980, p. 74) notes that even in the a-varieties, common words with the *ber-* verbal prefix, such as *berjalan* ('walk') and *bermain* ('play'), may be pronounced with no /r/.

2.1.7 The Lateral /l/

/l/ is always clear in native Malay words, so both tokens of /l/ in *lalu* ('then') are clear, and the final /l/ in *ambil* ('to take') is clear, even when it occurs before the *-kan* suffix in *mengambilkan* ('fetch') (Clynes & Deterding, 2011).

However, in words from Arabic, a dark /l/ may occur, particularly those words with a strong religious connotation such as *Allah* (Farid, 1980, p. 16; Mohd Azidan, 2004, p. 105). This creates a potential minimal pair for some speakers, as *Allah* [aɫah] contrasts with *alah* [alah] ('allergic'). On the basis of this finding one might conclude that /ɫ/ and /l/ are different phonemes, though the phonemic contrast between clear and dark /l/ would be hard to justify on the basis of a single minimal pair. Although dark /l/ occurs in words from Arabic such as *Kitabullah* ('the book of Allah'), which is a compound ending with *Allah*, it seems that other words from Arabic do not have dark /l/, including *ilmu* ('knowledge').

2.1.8 The Approximants /w/ and /j/

The approximants /w/ and /j/ occur in onsets, in words such as *wanita* ('woman') and *yang* /jaŋ/ ('which', 'who'), and also in codas, in words such as *pulau* /pulaw/ 'island' and *pandai* /pandaj/ 'clever'. Their occurrence in the coda assumes that syllable-final [aʊ] and [aɪ] are phonemically /aw/ and /aj/ respectively. This will be discussed in Section 2.2.1.

/u/ and /i/ are often reduced to [w] and [j] before a following vowel in fast speech, so *kuat* /kuat/ ('strong') can be [ku.ɐt˺] or [kwɐt˺], and *siapa* /siapa/ ('who') can be [si.ɐ.pɐ] or [sjɐ.pɐ]. This affects the syllable structure of words and allows for the possibility of word-initial consonant clusters, issues that will be discussed further in Section 2.3.

2.1.9 Phonemic Patterning

In terms of phonemic patterning, it is useful to consider further how the consonant table is represented. Although the columns of Table 1 refer to the passive articulator, as is normal for the IPA consonant chart, Clynes and Deterding (2011) suggest that the consonants phonemically pattern primarily in terms of the active articulator, as shown in Table 2.

Evidence that these are the relevant natural classes comes from morphophonemic alternations. Take, for example, the behaviour of *məN-*, the active voice prefix, where the 'N' is realized as a nasal segment homorganic with the initial consonant of the root:

Table 2 Phonemic patterning of the native consonants according to the active articulator

	Labial	**Apical**	**Laminal**	**Dorsal**
Plosive / Affricate	p b	t d	ʧ ʤ	k g
Fricative			s	h
Nasal	m	n	ɲ	ŋ
Trill		r		
Approximant	w		j	
Lateral		l		

before labials /m/, /p/, /b/, *məN-* is /məm/: *məN+buat* /məmbuat/ 'to make'

before apicals /n/, /t/, /d/, *məN-* is /mən/: *məN+darat* /məndarat/ 'to land'

before laminals /ʧ/, /ʤ/, /s/, *məN-* is /məɲ/: *meN+sewa* /məɲewa/ 'to rent'

before dorsals /k/, /g /, /h/, *məN-* is /məŋ/: *məN+gali* /məŋgali/ 'to dig'

An analysis that classifies /s/ as an 'alveolar' incorrectly predicts *məN+sewa* as */mənewa/ rather than the actual /məɲewa/ (the /s/ is deleted by a regular process). Furthermore, there is a phonetic overlap such that the consonants shown in the 'post-alveolar' column in Table 1 are often actually alveolar, and this becomes less important once the primacy of the active articulator is recognized. Evidence from consonant harmony (Adelaar, 1992), which limits co-occurrence of homorganic consonants in root morphemes, also works in terms of the active articulator categories and not the passive categories.

We might note that, according to Farid (1980, p. 14) and also Teoh (1994, p. 102), the *meN-* prefix should be shown as /məŋ/ on the basis that vowel-initial stems have /məŋ/; so, for example, *ambil* ('to take') becomes *mengambil* /məŋambil/ and *ikat* ('to tie') becomes *mengikat* /məŋikat/. We might alternatively say that *ambil* and *ikat* actually begin with a glottal stop, and a glottal stop can be regarded as dorsal, thereby predicting the *meng-* prefix; but this is inconsistent with the non-linear autosegmental analysis proposed by Teoh (1994), under which the glottal stop is unspecified for place of articulation.

2.2 Vowels

There are six vowel phonemes in Standard Malay: /i, e, a, o, u, ə/. Their quality can be represented as in the vowel plot in Figure 2 (Clynes & Deterding, 2011). This is similar to the quality of the vowels reported in Indonesian by Soderberg and Olson (2008), who suggest, however, that /ə/ is more close and a little more front.

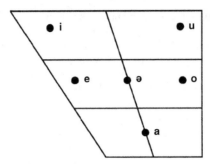

Figure 2 The quality of the six vowels of Malay.

Yunus (1980, p. 2) suggests that /a/ is an open front vowel, similar to Cardinal Vowel 4 [a], unlike the central quality suggested by Figure 2; and Indirawati and Mardian (2006, p. 35) and Abdul Hamid and Nurfarah (2013, p. 42) similarly claim that it is a front vowel. However, other studies indicate that it has a central quality, so it is not a front vowel. Farid (1980, p. 24) associates /a/ with the features $\begin{bmatrix} -front \\ -back \end{bmatrix}$, just like /ə/, confirming that it is a central vowel, while in contrast /i/ and /e/ are $\begin{bmatrix} +front \\ -back \end{bmatrix}$ and /u/ and /o/ are $\begin{bmatrix} -front \\ +back \end{bmatrix}$ respectively. Asmah (1991, p. 2) refers to /a/ as 'the low central vowel', Clynes and Deterding (2011) show it with an open central quality, and similarly for Indonesian, Soderberg and Olson (2008, p. 211) provide a vowel chart suggesting that /a/ has an open central quality. Here, we represent the phonetic quality of /a/ as [ɐ] (i.e. with a mid-open central quality).

In the a-variety, word-final /a/ sometimes has a raised allophone. This raising is probably an influence from the schwa-variety of Malay that is the standard in places such as Kuala Lumpur, Johor, and Singapore (Clynes & Deterding, 2011), and some speakers of the a-variety may adopt an intermediate quality, halfway between [ə] and [ɐ]. For the schwa-variety, Farid (1980, p. 21) asserts that the underlying phoneme for word-final [ə] in open syllables is /a/ which gets raised by the following rule (in which # represents a word boundary):

a→ə/_#

We should also note that word-final <a> is not always produced as [ə] even in the schwa-variety of Malaysian Malay. So this process of raising suggested by Farid (1980) should be regarded as representing a tendency rather than an absolute rule.

Apart from its realization of word-final <a> in schwa-varieties of Malay, /ə/ does not normally occur in final syllables, and this is true when there is a consonant in the coda of the final syllable. Where /ə/ occurs in non-final syllables, it is not usually given prominence, and it often undergoes ellipsis, so *sekarang* /səkaraŋ/ ('now') may be pronounced as [skɐrɐŋ], and *setuju* /sətudʒu/ ('agree') can be [studʒu] (Clynes & Deterding, 2011). Farid (1980, p. 92) proposes an ə-deletion rule that optionally deletes schwa in the initial syllable of a word which begins with a consonant and the following syllable starts with /r/, /l/, /n/, or /s/, giving forms such as *beras* /bəras/ ('rice') pronounced as [brɐs] and *belah* /bəlah/ ('to cut open') pronounced as [blɐh]. But it seems that this list of medial consonants allowing for the omission of /ə/ needs to be extended to include the omission of /ə/ in *sekarang* and *setuju*.

/i/ and /u/ contrast fully with /e/ and /o/ respectively only in penultimate syllables: *bila* /bila/ ('when') versus *bela* /bela/ ('defend'), and *dua* /dua/ ('two') versus *doa* /doa/ ('prayer').

In final closed syllables, /i/ and /u/ can have mid realizations, so *adik* ('younger sibling') can be [ɐdɪʔ] or [ɐdeʔ], while *ikut* ('to follow') can be [ikʊt˺] or [ikot˺], and Yunus (1980, p. 16) shows them with the more open vowel as /adeʔ/ and /ikot/ respectively. The realization of /i/ and /u/ as [e] and [o] in closed final syllables is the most usual pronunciation in Peninsular Malaysia. But for some other varieties, including the Standard Malay spoken in Brunei described in Section 5, the less open quality is found, so *terik* ('scorching') is [tərɪʔ] and *berambut* ('having hair') is [bərɐmbʊt˺] (see Appendix 1). Teoh (1994, p. 32) notes that these two vowels in final closed syllables could be analysed as /i/ and /u/ which get lowered, or they could be /e/ and /o/ which get raised. He prefers the first option on the basis that /i, u, a/, the vowels that can occur in closed final syllables, represent a more natural set of vowels than /e, o, a/. In fact, the spelling of words such as *adik* and *ikut* was shown with <e> and <o> in the *Ejaan Sekolah* ('School Spelling') system that was in use until 1975 (Teoh, 1994, p. 33). Some place names still reflect the old spelling, so Gadong and Temburong (places in Brunei) use this traditional spelling and would be Gadung and Temburung if they adopted the standard spelling system for Malay that is used today. Similarly, the reservoir in Brunei known as Tasek Lama would be Tasik Lama if the modern system of spelling were used. The mid vowels /e/ and /o/ on the other hand never have high allophones, so *pendek* ('short') is [pendeʔ] but never *[pendɪʔ], and similarly *pondok* ('hut') is [pondoʔ] and never *[pondʊʔ] (Clynes & Deterding, 2011).

In the orthography both /e/ (*e taling*) and /ə/ (*e pepet*) are represented as <e>, so in some cases the pronunciation of a word cannot be predicted from its spelling. For example, *perang* /peraŋ/ ('blond') and *perang* /pəraŋ/ ('war') are homographs but not homophones, as are *rendang* /rendaŋ/ ('bushy') and *rendang* /rəndaŋ/ ('stew'). This can give rise to confusion, as with *erat*, which some speakers pronounce as [erɐt˺] even though it is officially stipulated to be /ərat/, as discussed in Section 1.1.

2.2.1 Diphthongs?

Yunus (1980, p. 41) suggests that there are three diphthongs in Malay: [ai] (as in *pandai*, 'clever'), [au] (in *pulau*, 'island'), and [oi] (in *amboi*, 'expression of wonderment'). These always occur at the end of a syllable, and Farid (1980, p. 22) states that the second vowel in these sequences 'will be realized as syllable-margin'. Although [aɪ] and [aʊ] can occur non-finally in some words, such as *hairan* [haɪ.rɐn] ('surprised') and *walaupun* [wɐ.laʊ.pʊn] ('although'), they are always syllable-final. On this basis, the syllable-final phonetic diphthongs [aɪ], [aʊ], and [oɪ] can be treated phonologically as /aj/, /aw/, and /uj/ respectively; that is, as a monophthong vowel followed by an approximant (Clynes, 1997). Words like *baik* ('good') and *laut* ('sea'), in which the sequence of two vowels is followed by a consonant coda, consist of basically two syllables, even if they may be pronounced as a single syllable with a diphthong vowel by many speakers in conversational speech.

Asmah (1985), Zaharani (1993), and Clynes and Deterding (2011) all consider syllable-final diphthongs phonemically to be a monophthong followed by an approximant, and on this basis *pandai* is /pandaj/, *pulau* is /pulaw/, and *amboi* is /ambuj/. This is consistent with stating that a Malay syllable has the structure (C)V(C), an optional onset followed by an obligatory vowel and then an optional coda, though, as we mentioned in Section 2.1.3, Teoh (1994) suggests that the onset consonant is obligatory. The optional single consonant in the coda may be a voiceless plosive /p, t, k/, a nasal /m, n, ŋ/, a fricative /s, h/, or a liquid /l, r/, and it can also be an approximant /j/ or /w/; but there cannot be a combination of these, which explains why /aj/ and /aw/ can never be followed by a tautosyllabic consonant, so *baik* and *laut* are bisyllabic. Clynes (1997) argues that this V+C phonemic analysis of the diphthongs is appropriate for all Austronesian languages on the basis of a range of evidence, including alternations in Paiwan and omission of consonants in Kelantan Malay. In Paiwan, an Austronesian language spoken in Taiwan, there are alternations such as that between morpheme-final /w/ and /v/ (Clynes, 1997, p. 351); and in Kelantan Malay, Standard Malay *jual* /dʒual/ ('to sell') is /dʒua/ with no /l/, Standard Malay *kedai* /kədaj/ ('shop') is /kəda/ with /a/ instead of /aj/, and Standard Malay *pisau* /pisaw/ ('knife') is /pisa/ with /a/ rather than /aw/ (Clynes, 1997,

p. 356). So we can see that word-final /l/, /j/, and /w/ in Standard Malay are all omitted in Kelantan Malay.

An alternative analysis is offered by Teoh (1994, p. 135), who represents the diphthongs of Malay as a sequence of two vowels, and the second vowel becomes incorporated into the coda of the more sonorous first vowel. This, therefore, suggests that the underlying forms of [aɪ] and [aʊ] are /ai/ and /au/ rather than the /aj/ and /aw/ proposed by Clynes (1997).

In the widely accepted spelling system for Malay, it is important to differentiate the letters <ai> that occur in the same morpheme in words such as *pandai* ('clever') from the letters <ai> in which the <i> is the locative suffix *-i* in words such as *mulai* ('to start'). Phonemically, *pandai* is /pan.daj/ (bisyllabic), while *mulai* is /mu.la.i/ (trisyllabic), and the latter may be pronounced as [muleʔi] with a glottal stop separating the final two syllables. Under this analysis, every vowel represents the nucleus of a syllable, so the phonological sequence /ai/ must be two syllables. Unfortunately, the orthography fails to differentiate these two types of word-final <ai>, and this can lead to confusion (Sato, 2015, p. 5). Noor Azam Haji-Othman (personal communication) notes that there is some uncertainty about whether *memeterai* ('to endorse') is /məmətəraj/, which is pronounced as [məmətəraɪ] (with the <ai> in the same syllable), or /məmətərai/, which may be pronounced as [məmətərɐʔi] (with the <a> and the <i> in two different syllables).

2.3 Syllable Structure

More than 90 per cent of the native lexicon is based on bisyllabic root morphemes, with a small number of monosyllabic and trisyllabic roots (Adelaar, 1992). However, with widespread prefixing and suffixing, many words of five or more syllables are found. In the native lexis, the syllable structure is C_1VC_2, where both C_1 and C_2 are optional. C_1 can be any consonant, though /w/ and /j/ occur initially only in a few words, such as *wangi* /waŋi/ ('fragrant') and *yang* /jaŋ/ ('which'). In morpheme-final syllables, C_2 can be any consonant except the laminals /tʃ, dʒ, ɲ/ or the voiced plosives /b, d, g/.

In non-final syllables in the root morphemes of the native lexis, C_2 is usually either a nasal or /r/. Nasals in non-final position are homorganic with a following obstruent, except that /ŋ/ can precede /s/, as in *bangsa* /baŋsa/ ('ethnic group'). /r/ can occur before any consonant except /h/, /w/, or /j/; for example, in *bersih* /bərsih/ ('clean'), *terbang* /tərbaŋ/ ('fly'), and *kertas* /kərtas/ ('paper'). Teoh (1994, p. 58) notes that, although /ɲ/ cannot occur at the end of a word, it can occur at the end of a syllable in words such as *kunci* /kuɲtʃi/ ('key') and *janji* /dʒaɲdʒi/ ('to promise') as a result of being homorganic with the following /tʃ/ or /dʒ/.

In loanwords, other sonorants and obstruents also appear in non-final C_2 positions; for example, in *hairan* /hajran/ ('amazed') and *akhbar* /axbar/ ('newspaper'), which both originate from Arabic, and *saudara* /sawdara/ ('relative', 'sibling') from Sanskrit.

In the native lexis, any vowel except /ə/ can occur in morpheme-final syllables. Only /i/, /u/, and /a/ occur in final open syllables, though, as already discussed, /ə/ exists as the usual realization of <a> in final positions in the schwa-variety in words such as *bila* /bilə/ ('when'), though this is /bila/ in the a-variety. A rule of vowel harmony applies morpheme-internally to the non-central vowel phonemes /i/, /u/, /e/, and /o/. Where they occur in both the penultimate and final syllables, they must agree in height. So, we find *bilik* /bilik/ ('room') and *burung* /buruŋ/ ('bird') in which the vowels are the same, though, as we have seen, the second vowel often has a relatively open allophone: [bilɪʔ] ~ [bileʔ] and [burʊŋ] ~ [buroŋ]. We also find *hidung* /hiduŋ/ ('nose') and *rumit* /rumit/ ('complex'), in which the vowels differ in the front/back dimension but not the open/close dimension. If the first vowel is /e/ or /o/, then the second vowel must also be /e/ or /o/: *boleh* /boleh/ ('can') and *tengok* /teŋok/ ('to look'). Sequences of high and mid non-central vowels do not occur in either order, so */heduŋ/ and */bolih/ do not occur (Adelaar, 1992).

2.3.1 Clusters

Although word-initial and word-final consonant clusters cannot occur in the underlying phonemic representation, some sequences of consonants can occur in medial position, particularly involving a nasal followed by another consonant: /m/ + /p/ in *jumpa* /dʒumpa/ ('to meet'); /n/ + /t/ in *nanti* /nanti/ ('to wait'); /ɲ/ + /tʃ/ in *kunci* /kuɲtʃi/ ('key'); /ŋ/ + /s/ in *bangsa* /baŋsa/; and /ŋ/ + /g/ in *panggil* /paŋgil/ ('to call'). In all these examples, the first consonant is the coda of the first syllable, while the second consonant is the onset of the second syllable. In addition, a wide range of consonant clusters occur in the native lexis across morpheme boundaries before the verbal suffix *-kan*, as in *muatkan* /muatkan/ ('to fit in') and *sampaikan* /sampajkan/ ('to deliver'), and also before the possessive *-nya* suffix, as in *jubahnya* /dʒubɐhɲɐ/ ('his cloak'). Some loan words, such as *fitnah* ('slander') and *makna* ('meaning'), both of which originate from Arabic, have a plosive + nasal medial cluster; but such clusters involving a plosive followed by a nasal do not occur in the root morphemes of the native lexis.

Initial clusters occur only at the phonetic level as the result of optional ellipsis of /ə/ or reduction of /u/ and /i/ to [w] and [j]. Ellipsis of /ə/ is illustrated by *sekarang* /səkaraŋ/ [skɐrɐŋ] ('now') and *semakin* /səmakin/ [smɐkɪn] ('the more'). Omission of /ə/ can result in a three-consonant cluster; for example, the four syllables of *seterusnya* /sətərusɲa/ ('next') are sometimes pronounced as [strʊsɲɐ], with just two syllables, as we will see in Section 5.5. Initial clusters involving the approximants [w] and [j] occur as a result of the optional reduction of /u/ to [w] before a following vowel, as in *kuat* /kuat/ [kwɐt'] ('strong'), or the optional reduction of /i/ to [j] before a following vowel, as in *siapa* /siapa/ [sjɐpɐ] ('who') (Clynes & Deterding, 2011).

2.3.2 Geminates

Some varieties of Malay have geminate initial consonants. For example, in Pattani Malay (spoken in southern Thailand), /pagi/ ('morning') contrasts with /pːagi/ ('early morning'), and /dapo/ ('kitchen') contrasts with /dːapo/ ('in the kitchen') (Abramson, 2003). Hamzah, Fletcher, and Hajek (2011) analyse geminates in Kelantan Malay, which is closely related to Pattani Malay, and they report that the duration of the closure before the initial geminates in words such as /ppitu/ ('at the door'), /ttanɔh/ ('outside'), and /kkiɣi/ ('to the left') is substantially longer than before the corresponding singleton plosives in /pitu/ ('door'), /tanɔh/ ('land'), and /kiɣi/ ('left'), though the Voice Onset Time (VOT) following the release of the plosive is a little shorter for the geminates than the singletons. Teoh (1994, p. 132) analyses some initial geminates of Kelantan Malay as arising out of the loss of /ə/ and then assimilation of the initial /m/ from the *meN-* verbal prefix. He gives examples such as [bbəsaː] ('to grow big') which is the equivalent of Standard Malay *membesar*, and [ŋŋɔɣɛŋ] ('to fry') which in Standard Malay is *menggoreng*.

Standard Malay does not have this kind of initial gemination, but a potential medial geminate /k/ can occur when the verbal suffix *-kan* is attached to a root with a final /k/. Teoh (1994, p. 61) notes a potential contrast between *masakan* ('the cooking'), in which the nominalizing suffix *-an* is attached to the root *masak* ('to cook'), and *masakkan* ('cook!'), in which the *-kan* suffix is added to the stem to form an imperative verb (Liaw, 1999, p. 334). However, this distinction between *masakan* and *masakkan* is not always maintained in fast speech, and Teoh (1994, p. 63) notes that words such as *pertunjukan* ('the show') are often misspelt by students as **pertunjukkan*, suggesting a geminate consonant even though the suffix in this word is *-an* and not *-kan*. This potential contrast between singleton and geminate medial /k/ in Standard Malay will be investigated further in Section 5.1.

2.4 Stress

It has sometimes been stated that words in Malay and Indonesian have stress on the penultimate syllable, unless the penultimate syllable has a schwa, in which case the final syllable is stressed (Soderberg & Olson, 2008). However, others have questioned this claim. Zuraidah, Knowles, and

Yong (2008) and Clynes and Deterding (2011) assert that Malay has no lexical stress. Wan Aslynn (2019) collected data from speakers of standard Malay from the west coast of Peninsular Malaysia and measured the duration and amplitude of disyllabic words, trisyllabic words, and morphologically complex words with four syllables in isolation as well as in sentences. She has found no evidence for any of the syllables of these words being longer or louder, except that the final syllable was longer when the words were produced in isolation, which can be interpreted as phrase-final lengthening. For Indonesian, van Zanten, Goedemans, and Pacilly (2003) also conclude that there is no lexical stress, while Goedemans and van Zanten (2007, p. 35) note that stress can occur almost anywhere. Maskikit-Essed and Gussenhoven (2008) compared the duration of the penultimate syllable of words in Ambonese Malay with similarly structured words in Dutch, which uncontroversially does have lexical stress. They show that the penultimate syllable of words in Ambonese Malay is not longer than other syllables, so they conclude that there is no evidence for lexical stress in the language.

If there is little acoustic evidence to support the claim for lexical stress in Malay, why is it sometimes claimed that the penultimate syllable is stressed? A rise–fall pitch movement commonly occurs across the penultimate and final syllables of a phrase both in Malay (Zuraidah et al., 2008) and in Indonesian (van Zanten et al., 2003); and it seems that, when words are spoken in isolation, this can create an impression of penultimate word stress, especially when the final syllable is lengthened.

2.5 Rhythm

It was once claimed that all languages could be neatly categorized as stress-timed or syllable-timed (Abercrombie, 1967), though there would need to be more than two categories, as Japanese has mora-timing (Hoequist, 1983). However, based on acoustic measurements of duration, Roach (1982) raised fundamental doubts about classification into stress and syllable timing, and both Dauer (1983) and Miller (1984) suggested that rhythm of speech exists along a continuum rather than having fixed categories.

Despite these doubts about the existence of discrete rhythmic categories, more recent acoustic measurements have shown that it is possible to detect an acoustic distinction between different kinds of speech rhythm. Low, Grabe, and Nolan (2000) proposed a normalized Pairwise Variability Index (nPVI) that reflects the rhythmic classification of various languages based on a comparison of the vowels in successive syllables, as greater intersyllable variation in duration is found in stress-timed languages than in syllable-timed languages. Although a number of issues remain to be resolved in the implementation of the nPVI (Deterding, 2012; Fuchs, 2016), it has been successfully used to indicate the rhythm of a wide range of different languages (Grabe & Low, 2002).

Zuraidah, Knowles, and Yong (2008) note that the rhythm of Malay is sometimes claimed to be syllable-timed, but few attempts have been made to explore this in depth. Grabe and Low (2002) measured a single speaker of Malay in their investigation of the rhythm of 18 different languages, but their results for Malay were inconclusive. However, on the basis of reading of the North Wind and the Sun passage by six Malay and six British speakers, Deterding (2011) showed that there are substantial differences between the rhythm of Malay and English, with all of the Malay speakers exhibiting substantially more evenly timed syllables than the British speakers, suggesting that Malay might indeed be classified as more syllable timed than British English. Wan Aslynn (2012) analysed the rhythm of sentences read by 10 male and 10 female speakers of Standard Malay and reported that the measurements of nPVI confirm that Malay can be described as relatively syllable timed, though she noted substantial variation between the different speakers and also the different sentences that they read. Investigation of the rhythm of Malay will be discussed further in Section 5.6.

2.6 Intonation

There are three crucial elements to the description of intonation: how utterances are separated into chunks, sometimes called intonational phrases; what the prominent words are, the words that function as the anchor point for pitch movement; and how the pitch moves. Wells (2006, p. 6) refers to these three aspects of intonation as tonality, tonicity, and tone.

While the intonation of English has been widely described (e.g. O'Connor & Arnold, 1973; Wells, 2006), the intonation of Malay has not received so much attention. Zuraidah and Knowles (2006, pp. 508–9) note that sentences that are read aloud tend to begin with a high pitch with its peak at the end of the first word, but the extent to which the intonation of read speech is the same as that of conversational speech is unclear. Zuraidah and Knowles (2006) also report some detailed research on the intonational features adopted by speakers to hold or relinquish the floor in conversational interactions, showing that the completion of a speaker's turn is generally associated with a fall in pitch, and non-completion of a turn is marked by rising or level pitch. However, little has been done to describe how Malay utterances are broken into chunks, what the prominent words are and how they are signalled acoustically, what the inventory of intonational tones consists of, and how such tones are used.

Some work has been done on the intonation of Indonesian, but there still remains substantial uncertainty. For identifying tone unit boundaries (tonality), Odé (1997) reports that there was considerable variation between ten listeners in identifying the boundaries in two minutes of conversational data between two speakers; and furthermore, the listeners found it hard to identify which were the prominent words (tonicity). Indeed, of the 204 words in the conversation, all ten listeners were able to agree only on the existence of prominence on two of the words (p. 157). Ladd (2008, p. 61) suggests that the penultimate syllable in Indonesian provides the anchor point for intonational events, but it is not clear if all listeners hear such anchor points as prominent. Furthermore, Goedemans and van Zanten (2007, p. 39) claim that the penultimate syllable does not always function as the metrically strong anchor point for prominence at the phrase level.

Ebing and van Heuven (1997) suggest seven different patterns, four rises and three falls, stylized versions of which were regarded as reasonably acceptable by listeners, but the occurrence of these patterns in natural data is uncertain. Odé (1997) asked listeners to mark conversational data between two speakers with punctuation marks. On the whole, rising pitch was associated with commas, while falling pitch was associated with full stops, suggesting that rising tones indicate non-final information while falling tones indicate the end of an utterance (p. 163).

Odé (1997, p. 158) also reports that a prosodic boundary tends to occur after a prominent word; but this is not fixed, and in conversational data, 25 per cent of boundaries occurred after non-prominent words. In addition, she reports (p. 159) that there was substantial disagreement between listeners, as all 10 listeners could agree on the placement of a prosodic boundary only in 12 out of 54 cases, and 4 out of these 12 cases of agreement coincided with turn completions. As there was substantial disagreement between the listeners in identifying both the boundaries and the prominent words, this suggests that a comprehensive model of intonation has yet to be achieved.

Poedjosoedarmo (1986) reports on intonational patterns that are used with fronted topics in Indonesian. So, for example, in the following there is continuous rising intonation on *saya dapat hadiah itu*, and then there is rising and falling intonation on *di sekolah*, with the peak on the second syllable of *sekolah* (p. 9):

↗	saya	dapat	hadiah	itu	|	↗ di	sekolah ↘
	I	get	prize	that		at	school ('I got that
							prize at school'.)

She also notes (p. 5) that level intonation can occur on the second part of an utterance in which there is a fronted topic:

↗ cantik   sekali ↘ | → gadis itu →
beautiful very   girl that ('She's very
                                        beautiful, that girl.')

Zuraidah and Knowles (2006, p. 492) state that, in Malay:

> Patterns which mark the end of a major structure ('final' position) generally
> fall in pitch except in the case of questions, and those which end minor
> structures ('non-final' position) typically involve sustained pitch or perhaps
> a slight rise in pitch.

In Section 5.7, we will further consider the intonation of the Standard Malay
spoken in Brunei by describing some of the patterns that occur in read speech and
also in conversational interactions. However, it must be acknowledged that knowledge about the intonation of Malay is limited, particularly how it differs in
varieties of Malay. For example, the intonation of the Malay spoken in Brunei
differs from that in Sabah and Sarawak, and also from that in Peninsular Malaysia;
but there are no detailed descriptions of this variation. The intonation of different
varieties of Malay is a subject that would benefit from further research.

3 Varieties of Malay

Typically, communities in which Standard Malay and Indonesian are spoken are
multilingual and multiglossic (Sneddon, 2003). This means that a wide range of
regional varieties of Malay are spoken alongside the standard varieties, and they
are often mutually unintelligible.

Asmah (2008, pp. 54–66) provides a brief overview of the dialects of Malay
spoken in Johor, Melaka, Kedah, Perak, Pahang, Kelantan, Terengganu, Negeri
Sembilan, Sarawak, and Brunei as well as the Kedayan dialect that is spoken in
Brunei and elsewhere in northern Borneo. Here we will focus briefly on three for
which there are relatively rich sources of data – Kelantan Malay, Brunei Malay, and
Kedayan – to provide an indication of the kind of variation that exists in Malay.
Each of these varieties, and also many other varieties of Malay, merits detailed
analysis, which will not be attempted here. It is hoped that further research might
focus on the phonetics of the different dialects of Malay and the variation that
occurs in the way they are spoken by different people in a range of contexts, so that
a more comprehensive picture can emerge about the pronunciation of Malay.

3.1 Kelantan Malay

Kelantan Malay is spoken in the state of Kelantan in the north-east of the Malay
Peninsula, bordering on Thailand (see the map in Figure 1 in Section 1). Asmah

(1991) provides an overview of Kelantan Malay, and Teoh (1994, pp. 129–33) describes changes affecting the syllable coda as well as initial geminates arising out of affixation (as discussed in Section 2.3.2). Hamzah et al. (2011) analyse the acoustic features of initial geminates in Kelantan Malay words such as /ppagi/ ('early morning'), /ttidɔ/ ('sleep by chance'), and /kkabo/ ('a beetle'), and their study confirms that the geminate consonants /pp/, /tt/, and /kk/ are clearly differentiated acoustically from the singleton stops /p/, /t/, and /k/.

While the inventory of basic consonants in Kelantan Malay is the same as that of Standard Malay (Asmah, 1991, pp. 5–6), their distribution and realization is somewhat different. Final /r/ is absent (Asmah, 1991, p. 29), while in initial and medial positions, /ɣ/ occurs instead of /r/ (Asmah, 1991, p. 12). In final position, /l/ is omitted, so Standard Malay *tebal* ('thick') is /təba/ in Kelantan Malay (Asmah, 1991, p. 10), while words that have final /s/ in Standard Malay tend to have /h/ instead in Kelantan Malay, so *beras* ('rice') is /bəɣah/ (Asmah, 1991, p. 8). The only nasal found in final position is /ŋ/, and final /m/ and /n/ in Standard Malay are both pronounced as /ŋ/ in Kelantan Malay, so *minum* ('to drink') is /minuŋ/ and *jamin* ('to guarantee') is /dʒamiŋ/. However, /ŋ/ does not occur after open vowels, and instead the vowel is nasalized, so *abang* ('elder brother') is /abɛ̃/ while *ayam* ('chicken') is /ajɛ̃/ (Asmah, 1991, pp. 14–15). All final plosives are realized as a glottal stop in Kelantan Malay, so *sedap* ('delicious') is /sədaʔ/ and *ketat* ('tight') is /kətaʔ/. Finally, in some words, there is simplification of medial nasal + plosive clusters, so *sembahyang* ('to pray') is /səmajɛ̃/ (Asmah, 1991, p. 17).

In contrast with the six vowels of Standard Malay, Kelantan Malay has eight vowels that can be represented as /ɨ, ë, ɛ̈, ə, a, ʉ, ö, ɔ̈/. The front vowels /ɨ, ë, ɛ̈/ are not as front as the Standard Malay front vowels /i, e/, and the back vowels /ʉ, ö, ɔ̈/ are not rounded, in contrast with the rounded back vowels of most other dialects of Malay (Asmah, 1991, p. 19). It has been suggested that /ë, ɛ̈/ arise historically from the splitting of /e/, while /ö, ɔ̈/ arise from the splitting of /o/ (Asmah, 1991, p. 20). Being a non-schwa variety of Malay, word-final <a> is pronounced as a full vowel, so *apa* ('what') is pronounced as /apɔ̈/ (Asmah, 1991, p. 24), though this realization of word-final <a> is actually variable, as there is a subregion of Kelantan that is part of the schwa-zone (Asmah, 1991, p. 3).

One issue with listing eight vowels in Kelantan Malay is that, if *ayam* ('chicken') is /ajɛ̃/, then /ɛ̃/ would need to be treated as a phoneme, as would /ɛ̃/ in words such as *orang* ('person') pronounced as /ɔɣɛ̃/ (Asmah, 1991, p. 20). An alternative to listing these nasal vowels as phonemes would be to treat word-final velar nasal /ŋ/ as present in the underlying phonemic representation, and this /ŋ/ gets deleted by rule, following open vowels. If this approach is adopted, then the pronunciations of *ayam* and *orang* in Kelantan Malay with a nasalised final vowel should be shown in phonetic brackets: [ajɛ̃] and [ɔɣɛ̃].

Finally, words with the word-final diphthongs [aɪ] and [aʊ] of Standard Malay, which were analyzed as /aj/ and /aw/ in Section 2.2.1, are pronounced with monophthongs in Kelantan Malay, so *sampai* ('to reach') is /sampɛ/ while *hijau* ('green') is /hidʑa/ (Asmah, 1991, p. 22). As discussed in Section 2.2.1, this is one of the pieces of evidence presented by Clynes (1997) to argue for a vowel + consonant analysis of the diphthongs, as omission of final /j/ and /w/ in Kelantan Malay is consistent with the omission of other word-final consonants.

3.2 Brunei Malay

Brunei Malay is the dominant language spoken in Brunei, even though Standard Malay is promoted by the government and used in all official communication, for television and radio broadcasts, and in education (though, in reality, teachers often slip into Brunei Malay in order to connect better with their students). The domains of use of Standard Malay and Brunei Malay can be described as a kind of diglossia (Ferguson, 1959), with Standard Malay the H(igh) variety and Brunei Malay the L(ow) variety. McLellan et al. (2016, p. 12) note that 'although everyone learns Standard Malay in school and all can understand it, almost nobody uses it on a regular basis'.

Brunei Malay differs markedly from Standard Malay in its phonology, grammar, and lexis (Clynes, 2014), to the extent that some might regard it as a separate language (Martin, 1996). Based on the analysis of 1,916 words in a comparative list of words (DBPB, 2011), Deterding and Ho (2021, p. 8) report that there is a 72.3% level of shared lexicon between Brunei Malay and Standard Malay, which suggests that the two are closely related yet still distinct.

Salient features of the consonants of Brunei Malay are as follows: initial /h/ is absent, and /r/ is produced clearly as a trill or tap. As a result of the omission of initial /h/, *hutan* ('forest') in Standard Malay is /utan/ in Brunei Malay, and *hitam* ('black') is /itam/ (DBPB, 2007), and this omission of initial /h/ gives rise to the compound *orang+utan* ('forest person') as the name of the orangutan, the great ape that is found in Borneo. The clear enunciation of /r/ as a trill or tap makes Brunei quite distinct from the other widely spoken local dialect of Malay in Brunei, Kedayan (see Section 3.3).

Brunei Malay has only the three vowels /i, a, u/ (Clynes, 2014). Their quality is shown in Figure 3, which is adapted from the plot shown in Deterding and Ishamina (2017) with the scales modified to allow easy comparison with a similar plot for Standard Malay in Figure 14 (see Section 5.4).

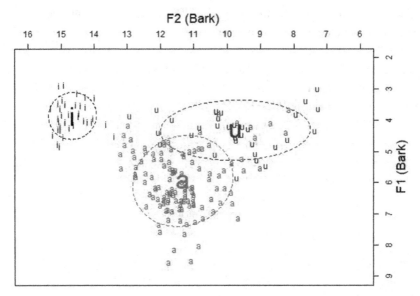

Figure 3 Quality of the three vowels of Brunei Malay from a reading of the North Wind and the Sun passage by a female speaker, adapted from the plot in Deterding and Ishamina (2017).

This sparsely filled vowel space allows for substantial variation in the pronunciation of the vowels, with a central allophone of /a/ occurring in many contexts, particularly in words that are more common in Standard Malay, such as in the first two syllables of *pangambara* ('traveller') that occurs in the North Wind and the Sun passage (Deterding & Ishamina, 2017).

The word-final diphthongs of Brunei Malay can be treated as vowel + approximant, just like in Standard Malay as discussed in Section 2.2.1. On this basis, a word like *paloi* ('stupid') might be treated as /paluj/, so it is unclear why it is spelled with <o> rather than <u> in the dictionary of Brunei Malay (DBPB, 2007). A further issue is that, for some speakers, *sikoi* ('melon') does not rhyme with *paloi*, as they end with [oɪ] and [uɪ] respectively (Deterding & Ishamina, 2017). If the vowels in the second syllables of *sikoi* and *paloi* are different, it is uncertain how this should be treated under the three-vowel analysis of Brunei Malay.

3.3 Kedayan

Kedayan is spoken by about 100,000 people in Brunei and neighbouring regions of Sarawak and Sabah. Nothofer (1991, p. 158) reports a level of 80% for lexical cognates between Standard Malay and Kedayan, confirming that they are closely related. Although Deterding and Ho (2021, p. 8) report a lower level of lexical cognates of 74% between Kedayan and Standard Malay than that claimed by Nothofer, nevertheless this level of shared vocabulary is sufficiently high to regard Kedayan as a dialect of Malay. Indeed, Asmah (2008, pp. 61–2) provides an overview of *Dialek Kedayan* in her encyclopedia of Malay, though she did not include Kedayan in her earlier survey of the phonology of Malay dialects (Asmah, 1991). Deterding and Ho (2021, p. 8) report that the level of shared lexicon between Kedayan and Brunei Malay is 88.1%, which confirms that these two varieties are closely related; yet at the same time they have features that make them distinct.

In contrast with Brunei Malay, initial /h/ occurs in Kedayan, so *hutan* is /hutan/ (Soderberg, 2014b; Faahirah & Deterding, 2019); and Kedayan has no /r/, so Standard Malay *merah* ('red') is /miah/ in Kedayan and *rumah* ('house') is /umah/ in Kedayan (DBPB, 2006, pp. 270 & 301).

Just like Brunei Malay, Kedayan has only three vowels, /i, a, u/ (Soderberg, 2014b). Figure 4 shows the acoustic quality of these three vowels, based on a reading of a passage by a female speaker (Faahirah & Deterding, 2019).

In comparison with the quality of the vowels of Brunei Malay shown in Figure 3, there appears to be less overlap between the open vowel and the other

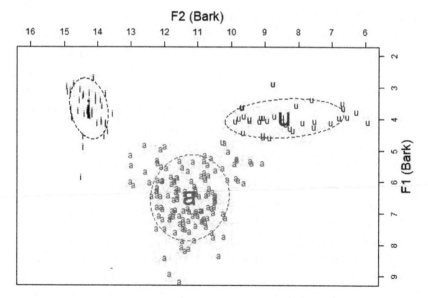

Figure 4 Quality of the three vowels of Kedayan from a reading of the North Wind and the Sun passage by a female speaker, adapted from the plot in Faahirah and Deterding (2019).

two vowels; but this conclusion should be treated with caution, given that it is based on the measurement of the vowels of a single speaker for each variety.

Soderberg (2014b) notes that words with /r/ in Standard Malay tend to have a lengthened vowel in Kedayan, so *bibir* ('lip') is /bibii/, *ular* ('snake') is /ulaa/, and *tidur* ('to sleep') is /tiduu/. On this basis, maybe we should conclude that the lengthened vowels should be shown as /i:, a:, u:/, and there are six vowels in Kedayan. Alternatively, we could state that word-final /r/ exists in the under-lying representation and is deleted by rule, or else that words such as /bibii/ are trisyllabic. Further research should look into the status of word-final lengthened vowels in Kedayan.

4 Materials for Research on Malay

In this section, we present some materials suitable for the analysis of Malay. First, we introduce a short text that can be read to facilitate analysis of the segments of Malay, particularly as it has been especially adapted to provide plenty of tokens of all the vowels of Malay. Then we introduce a Malay version of the map task that can be used to generate task-based conversational interactions between speakers. It is hoped that these two materials will be of value for other researchers who aim to investigate the pronunciation of Malay.

4.1 The North Wind and the Sun (NWS) Passage

The North Wind and the Sun (NWS) passage has traditionally been used by the International Phonetic Association for description of the pronunciation of different languages (IPA, 1999, p. 39). The passage is not ideal, as even for English, certain sounds such as /ʒ/ and word-initial /θ/ are missing (Deterding, 2006); but its continued use facilitates comparison between a wide range of different languages, including comparison between those language varieties that have been published as 'Illustrations' in the *Journal of the International Phonetic Association*. A version of this NWS passage has been used for the investigation of the phonetics of Standard Malay (Clynes & Deterding, 2011), Indonesian (Soderberg & Olson, 2008), Brunei Malay (Deterding & Ishamina, 2017), Kedayan (Soderberg, 2014b; Faahirah & Deterding, 2019), and Cocos Malay (Soderberg, 2014a).

It was decided to modify the passage to a certain extent from that used in Clynes and Deterding (2011). One aim of using the passage was to allow measurements of all six vowels of Malay in a range of contexts; but the direct translation of the passage that was used in Clynes and Deterding (2011) has only one token of /o/ (in *seorang* 'one person') and no tokens of /e/. It was therefore decided to augment the passage, adding a number of words with /e/ (*perang* 'blond', *merah* 'red', *boleh* 'can', *mereka* 'they', *helah* 'skill', *oleh* 'by', *berehat* 'rest', *lena* 'soundly', *rendang* 'bushy', *kecewa* 'disappointed', and *memang* 'still, actually') and also /o/ (*seorang* 'one person', *boleh* 'can', *sombong* 'proud', *oleh* 'by', and *pokok* 'tree'). Although the revised passage deviates somewhat from the original simple fable, and the rationale behind the traveller having blond hair and wearing a red cloak is not obvious, it is believed that it still reads well in Malay.

Of course, the passage is far from ideal. In particular, of the five marginal consonants of Malay, /f, v, z, ʃ, x/, only /x/ occurs, in *akhirnya* /axirɲa/ in line 9. The other four are relatively rare in ordinary Malay, and it would be challenging to include them all and still ensure the passage sounded natural.

4.1.1 Orthographic Version

The passage is shown below, with line numbers added for easy reference. The version read by the consultants in this research included no line numbers.

1 Ketika Angin Utara dan Matahari sedang bertengkar mengenai siapa yang
2 lebih kuat, seorang pengembara berambut perang yang memakai jubah
3 berwarna merah berjalan melalui tempat tersebut. Kedua-duanya
4 bersetuju bahawa siapa yang boleh menyebabkan pengembara itu
5 menanggalkan jubahnya, ia akan dianggap lebih kuat. Angin Utara dengan
6 sombong mengatakan ia yang paling kuat di antara mereka. Lalu Angin Utara
7 pun menghembuskan angin dingin yang sangat kencang. Namun semakin
8 kencang Angin Utara bertiup, semakin erat pula pengembara tersebut
9 membalut tubuhnya dengan jubah, sehingga akhirnya Angin Utara pun
10 mengalah. Kini tiba giliran Matahari menunjukkan helahnya. Dengan segera,
11 Matahari memancarkan sinarnya yang terik. Oleh sebab kepanasan,
12 pengembara tersebut menanggalkan jubahnya kemudian berehat lalu tertidur
13 lena ketika bersandar di sebatang pokok rendang yang berdekatan dengannya.
14 Walaupun kecewa akan kekalahannya, Angin Utara terpaksa mengakui
15 bahawa Matahari memang lebih kuat daripadanya.

A fairly literal English translation of this text is:

1 When the North Wind and the Sun were arguing about which was
2 the stronger, a traveller with blond hair wearing a cloak
3 that was red walked past that place. The two of them
4 agreed that whoever could cause the traveller to take off
5 his cloak, it would be regarded as the stronger. The North Wind
6 proudly claimed that it was the stronger of them. Then the North Wind
7 blew freezing air very powerfully. However, the more
8 powerfully the North Wind blew, the more closely the traveller

9   wrapped his body in the cloak, until finally the North Wind
10 conceded. Now it was the turn of the Sun to show its skills. Immediately,
11 the Sun shone out with rays that were scorching. Because of the heat,
12 the traveller took off his cloak before resting and falling asleep
13 soundly while leaning against a bushy tree that was near him.
14 Although it was disappointed over its failure, the North Wind had to admit
15 that the Sun was actually the stronger of the two of them.

4.1.2 Phonemic Transcription

In this phonemic transcription, we show commas as a minor discourse break '|'
and periods as a major break '||'. In reality, most readers are likely to break the
passage into more units than are suggested here, and this was indeed the case in
the recordings we made for this study.

1   kətika aŋin utara dan matahari sədaŋ bərtəŋkar məŋənai siapa jaŋ
2   ləbih kuat | səoraŋ pəŋəmbara bərambut peraŋ jaŋ məmakaj dʒubah
3   bərwarna merah bərdʒalan məlalui təmpat tərsəbut || kəduaduaɲa
4   bərsətudʒu bahawa siapa jaŋ boleh məɲəbabkan pəŋəmbara itu
5   mənaŋgalkan dʒubahɲa | ia akan diaŋgap ləbih kuat || aŋin utara dəŋan
6   somboŋ məɲatakan ia jaŋ paliŋ kuat di antara məreka || lalu aŋin utara
7   pun məŋhəmbuskan aŋin diŋin jaŋ saŋat kəɲtʃaŋ || namun səmakin
8   kəɲtʃaŋ aŋin utara bərtiup | səmakin ərat pula pəŋəmbara tərsəbut
9   məmbalut tubuhɲa dəŋan dʒubah | səhiŋga axirɲa aŋin utara pun
10 məɲalah || kini tiba giliran matahari mənuɲdʒukkan helahɲa || dəŋan səgəra |
11 matahari məmaɲtʃarkan sinarɲa jaŋ tərik || oleh səbab kəpanasan |
12 pəŋəmbara tərsəbut mənaŋgalkan dʒubahɲa kəmudian bərehat lalu tərtidur
13 lena kətika bərsandar di səbataŋ pokok rendaŋ jaŋ bərdəkatan dəŋaɲɲa ||
14 walawpun kətʃewa akan kəkalahaɲɲa | aŋin utara tərpaksa məŋakui
15 bahawa matahari memaŋ ləbih kuat daripadaɲa

In this transcription, *erat* ('close') in line 8 is shown as /ərat/, with *e pepet*,
following the stipulation of Dewan Bahasa dan Pustaka (as discussed in
Section 1.1), even though many speakers actually pronounce it as [erɛtˀ], with
e taling. Indeed, three out of four of our consultants pronounced it as [erɛtˀ] (see
Appendix 1).

   As discussed in Section 2.2.1, it is important for the phonemic transcription to
show the difference between the <ai> at the end of *mengenai* ('about') (line 1),
in which the <a> and <i> belong to different syllables, and the <ai> at the end of
memakai ('wear') (line 2), in which the <a> and <i> are in the same syllable. We
achieve this by using /ai/ for the former and /aj/ for the latter. As a result,

phonemically every syllable has one and only one monophthong vowel, so /ai/ represents the vowels in two separate syllables, and sometimes a glottal stop may be inserted between them [aʔi], while /aj/ represents the vowel and coda of a single syllable that is phonetically realized as the diphthong [aɪ]. Similarly, *walaupun* ('although') has three syllables, not four, so the medial syllable phonemically is /law/ which is phonetically pronounced as [laʊ].

Recordings of the NWS passage were made by four consultants: two females, F1 and F2, and two males, M1 and M2. Biographical details of these four consultants can be found in Appendix 1, which also includes a phonetic transcription of their reading of the text.

4.2 The Map Task

While recordings of a read text such as the NWS passage facilitate a detailed analysis of the consonants and vowels of Malay, we should be wary of basing the description entirely on a read passage, especially for the analysis of intonation, and it is important to consider spoken interactions (Zuraidah & Knowles, 2006). Here, we introduce a version of the map task that has been prepared for research on the pronunciation of Malay.

The map task is designed to generate conversational data between two speakers, each of whom has a map, and one of the maps has a route while the other does not. In addition, some of the landmarks differ. The two participants cannot see each other's map, and the task is for the one whose map has a route (the Leader) to guide the one whose map does not have a route (the Follower) along the path from *Mula* ('Start') to *Tamat* ('Finish'). Use of this map task is an excellent way to generate data that includes questions as the two participants negotiate the route while asking for clarification about their different landmarks (Anderson et al., 1991).

A version of the map task with the landmarks translated into Malay has been used to compare the intonation of English and Malay (Gut & Pillai, 2014). However, Faahirah (2014) found that the versions of the Malay maps used in that research were not ideal, because participants in Brunei had trouble with one of the landmarks (*Titik Triangulasi*, 'Trig Point') and furthermore there were rather a lot of words translated directly from English (*Padang Golf*, 'Golf Course'; *Pagar Piket*, 'Picket Fence'; *Tapak Karavan*, 'Caravan Park'; *Tapak Ujian Nuklear*, 'Nuclear Test Site'). A revised set of maps was therefore devised by Faahirah (2016) that only used landmarks that might be found in the local context in Brunei (e.g. *Hutan*, 'Forest'; *Rumah Panjang*, 'Longhouse'; *Air Terjun*, 'Waterfall'). The versions of the maps based on those of Faahirah (2014) and used in the current research are shown in Figure 5.

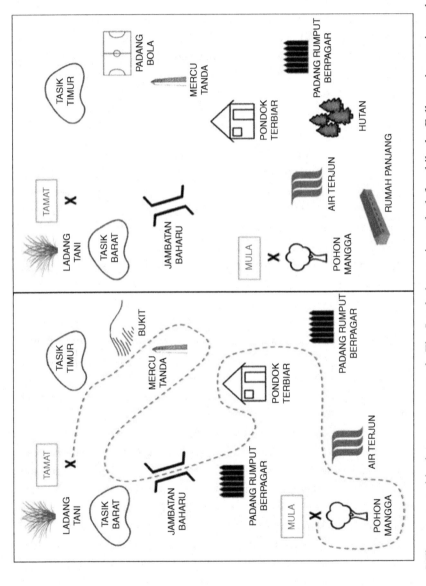

Figure 5 The maps used in the current research. The Leader's map is on the left, while the Follower's map is on the right. The task is for the Leader to guide the Follower from *Mula* ('Start') to *Tamat* ('Finish').

In discussing the map task data, the landmarks will be capitalized; so, for example, we refer to *Pohon Mangga* ('Mango Tree'), *Tasik Berat* ('West Lake'), and *Padang Rumput Berpagar* ('Fenced Meadow').

The recordings of the map task were made immediately after the consultants recorded the NWS passage. There were two map task recordings: one with F1 as the Leader and F2 as the Follower; and the other with M1 as the Leader and M2 as the Follower. The transcripts of the two map task recordings are included in Appendix 2.

5 Acoustic Analysis of the Pronunciation of Malay

Section 2 presented an overview of existing accounts of the pronunciation of Standard Malay. Here, we analyze the phonetics of Malay in continuous speech based on recordings of the NWS passage and also the map task by the four consultants, two females (F1 and F2) and two males (M1 and M2), all of whom are academics at Universiti Brunei Darussalam. They were chosen on the basis of their proficiency in Standard Malay and also their ability to keep to Standard Malay when talking to another Bruneian, which is rare in Brunei where it is more usual to converse in Brunei Malay (Martin, 1996; McLellan et al., 2016), something we wanted to avoid when obtaining conversational recordings for the analysis of Standard Malay. Brief biographical details of the four consultants are included in Appendix 1.

The recordings were made in a quiet office at Universiti Brunei Darussalam in April 2020. The NWS passage was recorded directly onto a laptop computer using a Samson C01U USB condenser microphone located a few inches from each speaker and saved in WAV format at 44.1 kHz sampling frequency. Phonetic transcription of the recordings of the NWS passage are provided in Appendix 1. The Map Task was recorded using a Zoom Handy H4n recorder with a bidirectional microphone placed between the two participants and saved in WAV format at 44.1 kHz sampling frequency. F1 was the Leader and F2 the Follower for the female map task recording, while M1 was the Leader and M2 the Follower for the male map task recording. Orthographic transcripts of the map task data are included in Appendix 2.

The main consultant for this research is M1, as he was available for frequent consultations before and after the recordings, and indeed he helped prepare the version of the NWS passage used here and also the Malay versions of the two maps for the map task. The detailed measurement of VOT for voiceless plosives and also the quality of vowels in the NWS passage are based on the recording by M1; but frequent reference is also made to the pronunciation of the other three consultants to ensure that the analysis of the pronunciation of Malay is not dependent on the idiosyncrasies of a single speaker.

5.1 Plosives

As expected, syllable-final /p/ and /t/ are generally unreleased, while /k/ at the end of a syllable is realized as [ʔ]. As discussed in Section 2.1.1, voiced plosives do not occur in final position in the native lexis, though they do occur in some borrowed words, for example *sebab* ('because') in line 11 of the NWS passage. In fact, all four consultants devoiced the final consonant in this word, and F2 unexpectedly released this final consonant, perhaps influenced by its Arabic origins. The release associated with this word-final plosive produced by F2 can be clearly seen in the middle of the spectrogram of a two-second extract in Figure 6. (For consistency of presentation, all spectrograms in this section will be for extracts that are exactly two seconds in duration. The time in seconds of the start of the extract from the beginning of the recording is shown on the left above the spectrogram, so in this case, the extract occurred about 55 seconds after the start. The frequency scale of all spectrograms is 0–5000 Hz.)

Initial /p/ and /t/ are always unaspirated, but there can sometimes be a small degree of aspiration associated with /k/ at the start of a syllable. In Figure 6 it can be seen that there is some aspiration after the /k/ in *kepanasan* ('heat'), but there is almost no aspiration following the /p/ in this word. Voice Onset Time (VOT) provides an indication of the degree of aspiration for plosives, and the VOT of the /k/ in this word is 33 msec while that of /p/ is 5 msec, confirming that there is a small amount of aspiration for the /k/ but almost none for the /p/.

The VOT of all syllable-initial voiceless plosives /p, t, k/ in the NWS passage was measured using Praat (Boersma & Weenink, 2020). For these measurements

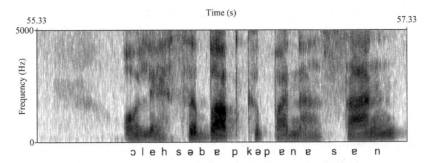

Figure 6 Spectrogram of a two-second extract of F2 saying *oleh sebab kepanasan* ('because of the heat').

of VOT, medial intervocalic consonants such as the /p/ in *kepanasan* are treated as syllable-initial. Indeed, Teoh (1994, p. 15) shows the structure of a word such as *ikat* ('to tie') as V$CVC, with $ indicating the syllable boundary, reflecting the fact that the /k/ in *ikat* functions as the onset of the second syllable, confirming that intervocalic plosives can be treated as syllable-initial.

Figure 7 shows the range of VOT for all the voiceless plosives in syllable-onset position in M1's reading of the NWS Text. All the tokens of both /p/ and /t/ have VOT less than 20 msec, confirming that there is little evidence of aspiration on any tokens of these two consonants, as aspirated plosives would typically have VOT of 60 msec or more in languages such as English (Docherty, 1992) and Chinese (Deterding & Nolan, 2007). The VOT of /k/ in the Malay NWS data is greater, with a range of 17 msec to 45 msec apart from one outlier (shown as an open circle) with VOT of 61 msec. The median (shown as a dark horizontal line in Figure 7) for /p/ is 13.5 msec, for /t/ it is 11 msec, and for /k/ it is 27 msec. The average VOT (not shown on the boxplot) for /p/ is 13.1 msec, for /t/ it is 11.0 msec, and for /k/ it is 28.8 msec.

The outlier for /k/ in the recording of M1 is for the token of *kuat* ('strong') that occurs in the final phrase of the NWS passage. The VOT for this token is measured at 61 msec; but in fact, even though this represents quite a long time delay from the release of the plosive to the start of voicing, which is how VOT is measured, the aspiration is minimal. The spectrogram in Figure 8 reveals that there is a clear burst of energy for the release of the closure in this word, but the level of energy following this burst up to the start of the vowel is quite weak, which is why this token of /k/ is not heard as aspirated. This illustrates that measurements of VOT sometimes do not reflect the full auditory perception of aspiration on plosives.

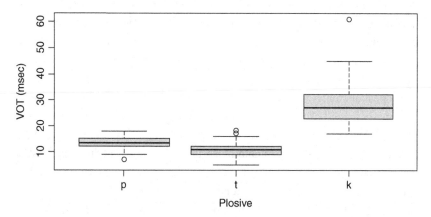

Figure 7 Boxplot of measurements of VOT for syllable-initial voiceless plosives in the NWS passage read by M1.

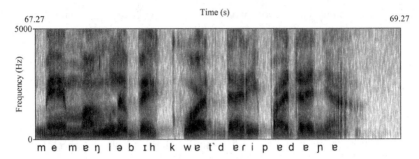

Figure 8 Spectrogram of M1 saying *memang lebih kuat daripadanya*
('actually stronger than him').

The other three consultants show similar patterns, with the VOT for /p/ and /t/ being under 20 msec in all cases, while /k/ has a greater range. In fact, some of the tokens of /k/ produced by F2 sound like they have a moderate degree of aspiration. Figure 9 shows a spectrogram of an extract from the recording of F2 in which the /k/ at the start of *kini* ('now') sounds fully aspirated. The VOT for this token of /k/ is 72 msec. One may note that the /t/ in *tiba* ('come') and *matahari* ('sun') in this extract have much less aspiration, with VOT of 18 msec and 13 msec respectively.

In Section 2.3.2, it was suggested that some speakers make a distinction between *masakkan* ('cook!') with geminate /k/ and *masakan* ('cooking') with singleton /k/. In line 10 of the NWS passage, there is a potential geminate /k/ when the verbal *-kan* suffix occurs in *menunjukkan* ('show'), for which the root is *tunjuk* ('to show'); and this can be compared to the singleton /k/ in *mengatakan* ('say') in line 6, in which the final suffix *-kan* occurs after the root *kata* ('to say'). For M1, the duration of the closure for the potential geminate /k/ in *menunjukkan* is actually a little shorter (58 msec) than the singleton /k/ in *mengatakan* (79 msec), and it is substantially shorter than the closure for the two plosives /bk/ in *meyebabkan* ('cause') in line 4 (99 msec). It seems, therefore, that M1 does not have a geminate /k/ in *menunjukkan*. Of the other three speakers, only M2 exhibits a longer closure in *menunjukkan* (98 msec) than *mengatakan* (73 msec), and even for him, the duration of the closure in *menunjukkan* is less than for the /bk/ in than *menyebabkan* (118 msec). Teoh (1994, p. 45) states that geminate stops tend only to occur in careful, slow speech, and it is normal for degemination to occur in fast speech in Standard Malay. It seems that this degemination is true for *mununjukkan* in the reading of the NWS passage by three out of four of our consultants, even though reading a passage might be regarded as careful speech.

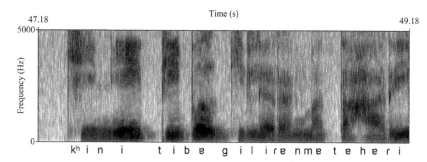

Figure 9 Spectrogram of F2 saying *kini tiba giliran matahari* ('now came the turn of the sun').

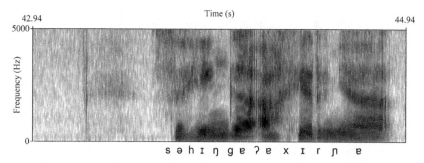

Figure 10 Spectrogram of F2 saying *sehingga akhirnya* ('until finally').

5.2 Fricatives

Of the five marginal fricatives of Malay /f, v, z, ʃ, x/, only the velar fricative /x/ occurs in the NWS passage, in *akhirnya* /axirɲa/ ('finally'). Figure 10 illustrates F2 saying the phrase *sehingga akhirnya* ('until finally'), and the /x/ in *akhirnya* is distinct from the /h/ in *sehingga*, with the /x/ having more intense energy at 2500 Hz.

However, /x/ is sometimes pronounced as [h], particularly in common words such as *akhirnya*. Of the four consultants, only F2 and M2 make a clear distinction between the /x/ in *akhirnya* and the /h/ in *sehingga*, while F1 and M1 have [h] in both words.

For final /h/, in the NWS passage there are 13 instances of /h/ occurring at the end of a syllable: *lebih* ('more') in lines 2, 5, and 15, *jubah* ('cloak') in lines 2 and 9, *jubahnya* ('his cloak') in lines 5 and 12, *merah* ('red') in line 3, *boleh* ('can') in line 4, *tubuhnya* ('his body') in line 9, *mengalah* ('concede') in line 10, *helahnya* ('its skills') in line 10, and *oleh* ('by') in line 11. In most cases, the /h/ is clearly produced. Figure 11 shows F1 saying *jubah* ('cloak') and

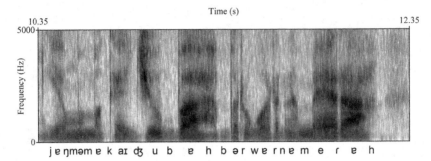

Figure 11 Spectrogram of F2 saying *yang memakai jubah berwarna merah* ('who was wearing a cloak that was coloured red').

merah ('red') with a clear /h/ at the end of each word. In each case, the formant structure of the preceding vowel continues during the /h/ but with reduced intensity, so one might characterize final /h/ as a voiceless end to the vowel, in this case [e̥].

However, syllable-final /h/ may be omitted in relatively common words. In the NWS passage, F1 omits the /h/ in *boleh* ('can') and *oleh* ('by'), and M2 omits the /h/ in the first token of *lebih* ('more', line 5) and also *oleh*. The final /h/ in *lebih* in the last phrase of the passage spoken by M1 is also fairly marginal, though maybe it is not entirely omitted (see the spectrogram in Figure 8 in Section 5.1).

5.3 /r/

There are 46 instances of /r/ in the NWS passage, and Table 3 shows their realization by each of the four consultants. While all four use a tap in the overwhelming majority of cases, F2 produces more instances of a trill than the other three, perhaps influenced by her background as a professional newsreader. In addition, she never omits /r/ as the others sometimes do, and both F2 and M2 use an approximant less often than the other two.

Figure 12 is a spectrogram of an extract from the recording of M1, showing the trilled /r/ at the start of *rendang* /rendaŋ/ ('bushy'), the only time he has a trilled /r/. One possibility in this case is that he was putting special emphasis on this word in order to ensure that he differentiated it from the homograph *rendang* /rəndaŋ/ ('fried'), and this led to careful enunciation in which he used a trill. In subsequent discussions, M1 agreed with this interpretation. Figure 12 also illustrates the occurrence of an approximant [ɹ] at the end of the first and third syllables of *bersandar* ('lean'), though it is hard to be sure that the /r/ is not omitted in these cases. Although at the end of this word there is the suggestion

Table 3 Realization of /r/ in the NWS passage by the four consultants

Speaker	Tap	Trill	Approximant	Omitted
F1	28	5	7	6
F2	34	11	1	0
M1	29	1	7	9
M2	37	6	1	2
Total	128 (69.6%)	23 (12.5%)	16 (8.7%)	17 (9.2%)

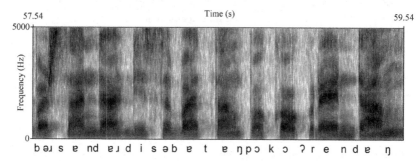

Figure 12 Spectrogram of M1 saying *bersandar di sebatang pokok rendang* ('leaning against a bushy tree').

of a dipping third formant, the usual acoustic diagnostic for [ɹ] (Hayward, 2000, p. 167), there is no evidence of a dipping third formant in the first syllable (though the fourth formant clearly does fall), so maybe this token of /r/ should be classified as omitted instead of an approximant.

Typically, /r/ may be omitted in prefixes such as *ber-* and *ter-* before a consonant, particularly in common words; so, for example, in line 3 of the NWS passage, M1 pronounces *berjalan* ('walk') as [bədʒɐlɐn] and *tersebut* ('the said') as [təsəbʊtˈ]. This is consistent with the observation of Yunus (1980, p. 74) that *berjalan* may be pronounced with no /r/. (In contrast, both F1 and M2 have a tap in this word, and F2 has a trill.) Figure 13 illustrates the absence of /r/ in *terpaksa* ('had to') from line 14 in the recording of M1, and also a clear occurrence of a tapped medial /r/ in *utara* ('north').

Twenty-six of the tokens of /r/ in the NWS passage are in intervocalic position, particularly in the six tokens of *utara* ('north') and four tokens of *matahari* ('sun'), but also in words such as *merah* ('red') and *terik* ('scorching'); 17 are before another consonant, mostly involving the *ber-* or *ter-* verbal prefixes in words such as *berjalan* ('walk') and *tersebut* ('the said'), but also in *sinarnya* ('its rays') and *memancarkan* ('shine'); two are in word-final position,

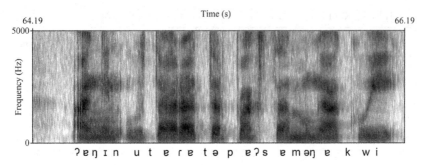

Figure 13 Spectrogram of M1 saying *angin utara terpaksa mengakui* ('the north wind had to admit').

bersandar ('lean') and *bertengkar* ('argue'); and just one is in initial position, in *rendang* ('bushy'). Table 4 shows the realization of all 184 tokens of /r/ in the four readings of the passage according to their position in the words.

A tap is particularly common for /r/ in intervocalic position, including every single instance of /r/ in the six tokens of *utara* ('north') and the four tokens of *matahari* ('sun') by all four speakers. A trill occurs in 12.5% of cases, particularly in *rendang* ('bushy') for three of the speakers and also the two instances of preconsonantal /r/ in *berwarna* ('coloured') by both F2 and M2, though it should be admitted that it is hard to be certain whether a tap or a trill occurs in some cases. An approximant occurs in nearly 9% of cases, and /r/ is omitted in a little over 9% of cases, all of them in preconsonantal context, particularly in *tersebut* ('the said'), though, just as with the pre-consonantal /r/ discussed in connection with *bersandar* in Figure 12, it is often difficult to determine with confidence whether word-final /r/ is omitted or realized as an approximant.

The map task recordings allow us to consider the realization of /r/ in conversational data and also in a wider range of contexts. In particular, two of the landmarks have an initial /r/, *Rumah Panjang* ('Longhouse') and *Padang Rumput Berpagar* ('Fenced Meadow'). There are a total of 207 instances of /r/ in the map task data, and their realization is shown in Table 5. The four instances of 'other' are all by F1: in one case, she pronounced *berada* ('there is') as [bəʔɐdɐ] with a medial glottal stop; and in three cases, she pronounced the *mercu* in *Mercu Tanda* ('Landmark') as [məsʧu]. It is unclear why this unexpected pronunciation of *mercu* occurred.

These figures confirm that a tap is the most common realization of /r/ in conversational data as well as read data, though the incidence of a tap at just over 50% is somewhat less than the nearly 70% reported for the NWS passage in Table 4. In contrast, there are more approximants (17.9% vs.

Table 4 Realization of /r/ in the NWS passage according to context

Context	Tap	Trill	Approximant	Omitted
Intervocalic	96	5	3	0
Pre-consonantal	30	12	9	17
Word-final	2	3	3	0
Word-initial	0	3	1	0
Total	128 (69.6%)	23 (12.5%)	16 (8.7%)	17 (9.2%)

Table 5 Realization of /r/ in the map task according to context

Context	Tap	Trill	Approximant	Other	Omitted
Intervocalic	61	5	17	1	1
Pre-consonantal	24	14	4	3	24
Word-final	14	9	11	0	5
Word-initial	5	4	5	0	0
Total	104 (50.2%)	32 (15.5%)	37 (17.9%)	4 (1.9%)	30 (14.5%)

8.7%) and omission (14.5% vs. 9.2%). In particular, an approximant sometimes occurs intervocalically, such as in three tokens of *terus* ('continue') by M1 and four tokens of *seterusnya* [stɹusɲɐ] ('continuing') by F1, though in the latter it is actually part of an initial cluster [stɹ] that occurs as a result of omission of /ə/ typical in conversational speech (to be discussed in Section 5.5).

5.4 Vowel Quality

In order to provide an acoustic description of the range of the quality of the vowels of Malay in context, the first two formants (F_1 and F_2) of all vowels in the recording of the NWS text by M1 were measured using Praat (Boersma & Weenink, 2020). The formant values in hertz were then converted to a Bark scale so that distances between formants roughly correspond to perceptual differences (Hayward, 2000, p. 141). The Bark values were calculated using the formula suggested by Traunmüller (1990), where the Bark scale value (z) is related to the frequency in hertz (f) by the formula:

$$z = 13 \; arctan(\, 0.00076f\,) + 3.5 \; arctan\left(\tfrac{f}{7500}\right)^{2}.$$

Values were calculated using R (R Core Team, 2016). The values of F_1 and F_2 were then plotted on inverted axes to show the quality of the vowels, with F_1 on

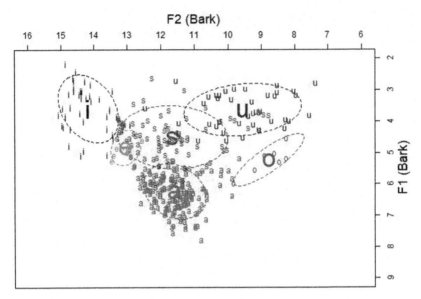

Figure 14 The vowels of M1 in the NWS text. The schwa /ə/ is labelled as 's'.

the y-axis to reflect the open-close quality and F_2 on the x-axis to represent the front-back dimension, as is usual in plots of vowel quality (Ladefoged & Johnson, 2011). Ellipses were drawn based on a bivariate normal distribution to encircle 68% of the tokens of each vowel, representing plus or minus one standard deviation (McCloy, 2012). The vowels of M1 from the NWS text are shown in Figure 14, which indicates that the vowels of M1 are fairly well separated in terms of quality, though there is some overlap between /ə/ (shown as 's' in Figure 14) and /e/, /a/, and /u/. This is because /ə/ is often very short, so it tends to undergo coarticulation with neighbouring consonants.

In Section 2.2, it was suggested that /i/ and /u/ in closed final syllables can have a mid allophone. This can be shown as [ɪ] and [ʊ] respectively, so *terik* ('scorching') (line 11 of the NWS passage) is [tərɪʔ] while *namun* ('but') (line 7) is [nɐmʊn]. Figure 15 shows all the tokens of /i/ and /u/ in final closed syllables as 'I' and 'U' respectively, and it can be seen that the quality is generally less close than that of other tokens of these two vowels.

5.5 Syllable Structure

In some words, two syllables in the underlying phonemic representation may actually be pronounced as a single syllable. For example, *kuat* /ku.at/ ('strong') in the NWS passage is mostly said as [kwɐt]. In line 14 of the passage, *mengakui* /məŋ.a.ku.i/ ('admit'), for which the stem is *aku* ('I'), is pronounced

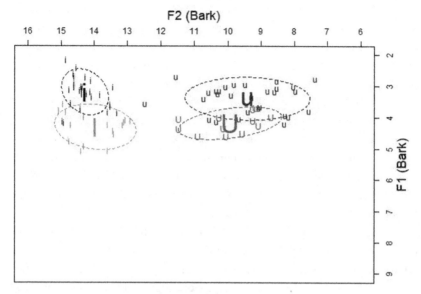

Figure 15 The mid allophones of /i/ and /u/ in the recording of the NWS passage by M1. All tokens of /i/ in closed final syllables are labelled as 'I', while those of /u/ in closed final syllables are shown as 'U'.

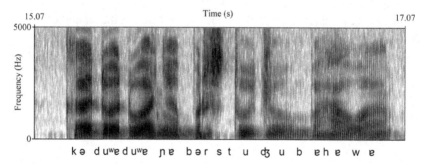

Figure 16 Spectrogram of M2 saying *kedua-duanya bersetuju bahawa* ('the two of them agreed that').

as three syllables [məŋ.ɐ.kwi] by all four consultants. In subsequent discussions, M1 confirmed that *mengakui* would be four syllables in careful, deliberate speech, but is generally three syllables in connected speech.

There may also be loss of a syllable when the schwa is omitted after /s/ in a word such as *bersetuju* ('agree') /bərsətudʒu/ or *semakin* ('the more') /səmakin/. Figure 16 shows a spectrogram of M2 pronouncing *bersetuju* (line 4) as [bərstudʒu], with no vowel between the [s] and [t].

In fact, all four consultants produce *bersetuju* with just three syllables, omitting the vowel after the /s/, and two of them (M2 and F2) produce both tokens of *semakin* (lines 7 and 8) as [smɐkɪn] with just two syllables, though the other two have a short vowel after the /s/ in this word, with an average duration of 20 msec. However, none of the four consultants omits the vowel in the first syllable of *sebatang* ('one MW', where *batang* is the measure word for trees) (line 13), and the average duration for the schwa in this word is 27 msec. It seems likely that omission of the vowel between /s/ and a following consonant is more frequent in relatively common words such as *bersetuju* than less common words such as *sebatang*. We should also note that the *se-* prefix in *sebatang* is a morpheme meaning 'one', and this may inhibit the omission of the vowel.

The word *seterusnya* /sətərusɲa/ ('next') occurs five times in the map task data, four times in the female recording and once in the male; and in all five tokens, it is pronounced [stɹʊsɲɐ], so one can say that the /ə/ in both the first two syllables is omitted, and phonetically the word begins with the three-consonant cluster [stɹ]. The spectrogram in Figure 17 illustrates the pronunciation of *seterusnya* as [stɹʊsɲɐ] by F1.

The omission of schwa in a word, resulting in word-initial consonant clusters, occurs elsewhere in the map task data. Figure 18 illustrates F1 saying *kawasan* /kawasan/ ('area') as [kwɐsɐn], with an initial [kw] cluster.

Of course, there are a range of processes that result in the simplification of pronunciation in conversational speech, and sometimes whole syllables are omitted, not just the vowel. Figure 19 illustrates M1 saying *jadinya* /dʒadiɲa/ ('so') as [diɲɐ] with the whole of the first syllable omitted.

Further research might investigate in greater depth the conditions under which syllables are reduced and omitted in conversational speech.

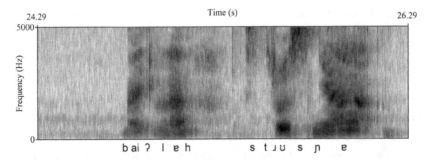

Figure 17 Spectrogram of F1 saying *baiklah seterusnya* ('OK, next') during the female map task recording.

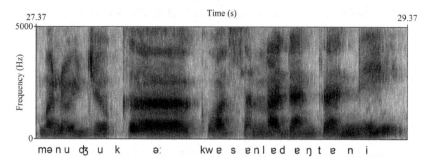

Figure 18 Spectrogram of F1 saying *menuju ke kawasan Ladang Tani* ('towards the area of the Farmed Land') during the female map task recording.

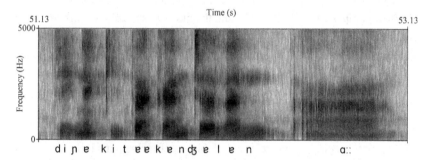

Figure 19 Spectrogram of M1 saying *jadinya kita akan jalan* ('so we will walk') during the male map task recording.

5.6 Rhythm

Measurements of the rhythm of Malay were obtained using the nPVI (Low, Grabe & Nolan, 2000), which derives an estimate of the rhythm of a phrase by comparing the duration of each vowel with that of the vowel in the next syllable and dividing the difference by the average of the two, using the formula

$$nPVI = 100 \times \frac{1}{m-2}\left[\sum_{k=1}^{m-2}\left|\frac{d_k - d_{k+1}}{(d_k + d_{k+1})/2}\right|\right]$$

where d_k is the duration of the kth syllable, and m is the number of syllables in the phrase.

Following the discussion in Deterding (2012), two adjustments from the nPVI as proposed by Low et al. (2000) were adopted:

- in order to mitigate the effects of utterance-final syllable lengthening, the final syllable was excluded from the calculation (so the formula only extends to *m-2*, comparing the duration of the antepenultimate syllable with the penultimate)
- the minimum duration of a vowel was set at 30 msec

The extent of final syllable lengthening may be more prevalent in English than other languages (Berkovitz, 1984). Therefore, as the results of the measurement of rhythm for Malay will be compared with similar measurements for English, it is best to eliminate the problem by discounting the final syllable.

It is important to adopt a minimum duration for vowels, as otherwise the results can be substantially affected by small differences in the measurement of consecutive short syllables. For example, in the NWS text, there are four tokens of *pengembara* ('traveller'), and the first two syllables of this word can have very short vowels. If the vowel in the first of these syllables has a duration measured at 10 msec and the second is 20 msec long, then comparison of their duration suggests a high level of variability, as the second vowel is twice as long as the first, when in fact there is little rhythmic variability, as both vowels are very short. This issue is resolved by using 30 msec as the minimum vowel duration. This strategy also deals with the issue of what to do when there is no obvious vowel in a syllable, as often happens following [s] in words such as *bersetuju* ('agree') [bərstudʒu] and *semakin* ('the more') [smɐkɪn].

Following the suggestions of Fuchs (2016), only utterances of at least six syllables were analysed. For example, M1 produced *lalu* ('then') (line 6), *namun* ('but') (line 7), and *dengan segera* ('immediately') (line 10) as independent phrases, so these three phrases were all excluded from the measurements of the rhythm of M1.

Two further methodological issues need to be addressed when measuring the rhythm of the Malay data: how to deal with /r/; and how to handle phonologically bisyllabic sequences such as that in *kuat* ('strong') which are often realized phonetically as [kwɐtˀ], with just one syllable.

As /r/ is a consonant, it should be excluded from the measurement of vowels. However, this is problematic when postvocalic /r/ is realized as the approximant [ɹ], as there is often no clear end to the vowel and start of the [ɹ]. This is further exacerbated by the fact that, as discussed in Section 5.3, it is often not possible to be certain about whether /r/ in postvocalic position is realized as [ɹ] or omitted. In situations such as this, any postvocalic [ɹ] is included in the duration of the vowel. There is a further problem when postvocalic /r/ is

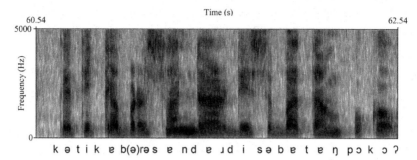

Figure 20 Spectrogram of F1 saying *ketika bersandar di sebatang pokok* ('while leaning against a tree').

realized as a trilled consonant [r], as the sound often occurs during the vowel, which then continues afterwards. For example, Figure 20 shows a spectrogram of an extract in which F1 utters *bersandar* ('leaning') with a trilled /r/ in the first syllable. Note that the [r] actually occurs near the [b], so it might be transcribed as [bərəsɛndeɹ] or even [brəsɛndeɹ]. In situations such as this, the measurement of the duration of the vowel includes the [r].

The analysis of words such as *kuat* is problematic because, although it is regarded as bisyllabic in a phonemic analysis and so the /u/ and /a/ should be measured as two separate vowels, phonetically it is generally (but not always) realized as a single syllable. It was decided to treat all instances of *kuat* as bisyllabic and to take the midpoint of the [ua] sequence as the end of the first syllable and start of the second syllable. It should be acknowledged that this tends to overestimate the syllabic timing of an utterance (Deterding, 2011), as it results in a sequence of two consecutive evenly timed syllables. However, it is best to avoid making subjective decisions about whether there are one or two syllables in a word such as *kuat*, as objective decisions such as this would have a major impact on the results.

Three of the speakers read the NWS passage with 26 phrases (excluding short phrases such as *namun*, 'but', and *dengan segera*, 'immediately' by M1), while F2 had 28 phrases. The nPVI of all these phrases was measured independently by the first two authors, here referred to as R1 and R2, and then their results were compared. There was disagreement of 10 msec or more over the duration of about 20.5% of the syllables, and in all these cases, both researchers reconsidered their measurements, and in many cases one or both of them adjusted their values.

Table 6 shows the final results of the nPVI measurements for the four consultants by the two researchers, R1 and R2, as well as the results for the

Table 6 Measurements of nPVI for the four Malay speakers by the two raters, R1 and R2, compared with similar measurements for six speakers of British English, B1 to B6, reported in Deterding (2011)

Speaker	nPVI (R1)	nPVI (R2)	Speaker	nPVI
F1	41.79	41.25	B1	57.39
F2	44.11	46.77	B2	64.09
M1	34.83	36.84	B3	55.51
M2	35.15	34.58	B4	63.74
			B5	62.18
			B6	56.20
Average	38.82	39.86		59.85

six speakers of British English, B1 to B6, reading the NWS passage reported in Deterding (2011). It can be seen that there is good agreement between R1 and R2, with both researchers finding that F2 has the highest value of nPVI, suggesting she has the least syllable-timed rhythm, while M1 and M2 have the lowest values, and the values for all the Malay speakers are less than those for all of the British speakers, indicating less variation between the duration of vowels in successive syllables in the Malay data and thereby confirming that Malay is more syllable-timed than British English. For R1, the average of 38.82 for the Malays is significantly different from the value of 59.85 for the British speakers ($t = 7.64$, $df = 5.92$, two-tailed, independent samples, unequal variance, $p < 0.001$), and for R2 the average of 39.86 is similarly significantly different from that of the British speakers ($t = 6.39$, $df = 5.12$, two-tailed, independent samples, unequal variance, $p < 0.001$). The results for Malay are almost the same as the average nPVI of 40.91 reported for Malay in Deterding (2011), and they are fairly similar to (but a little lower than) the results of Wan Aslynn (2012), who reports an average nPVI value of 44.8 for twenty speakers reading ten standard Malay sentences.

The boxplot in Figure 21 shows the range of values for the individual phrases by the four speakers in the measurements by R1, confirming that the median for F2 (43.23) is slightly higher than that of the other three speakers, while the medians for M1 (39.10) and M2 (39.35) suggest more syllable-timed rhythm for those two speakers. F2 has the greatest range of values, extending from 17.12 to 75.53, with this variability in rhythm perhaps reflecting her background as a newsreader.

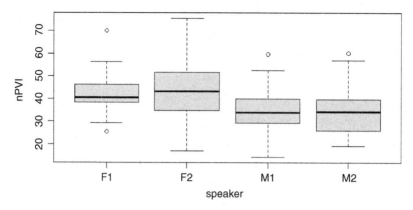

Figure 21 Boxplot of the values of the nPVI for the individual phrases produced by the four speakers.

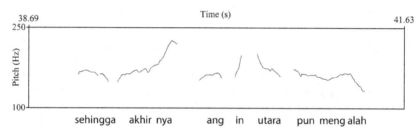

Figure 22 Pitch track of M1 saying *sehingga akhirnya, angin utara pun mengalah* ('until finally, the North Wind gave up').

5.7 Intonation

In the recordings of the NWS passage, non-final phrases usually end with rising pitch, while final phrases tend to have falling pitch. Figure 22 shows the pitch track of an extract from M1's recording in which there is a clear rise on *akhirnya* ('finally') at the end of the adverbial initial phrase and a fall on *mengalah* ('gave up') at the end of the second phrase. For both of these pitch movements, the anchor point, the place where the distinctive pitch movement begins, is the penultimate syllable in the phrase. In some accounts of Malay, this anchor point for the pitch movement would be described as the stressed syllable.

Similarly, F2 mostly (but not always) produces final phrases with falling intonation anchored on the penultimate syllable of the last word, while non-final phrases have a rising tone. The utterance whose intonation is shown in Figure 23 has two intonational phrases, the first one ending after *tersebut* ('the said'), and

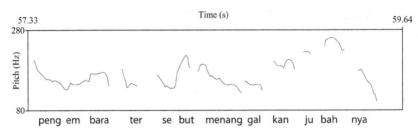

Figure 23 Pitch track of F2 saying *pengembara tersebut menanggalkan jubahnya* ('the traveller took off his cloak').

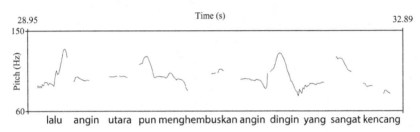

Figure 24 Pitch track of M2 saying *lalu angin utara pun menghembuskan angin dingin yang sangat kencang* ('then the north wind blew freezing air very powerfully').

there is a rise on this word occurring on the third (last) syllable, as the penultimate syllable has /ə/ which cannot be the anchor point for a tone, while the fall at the end of the utterance is anchored on the penultimate (second) syllable of *jubahnya* ('his cloak').

Although M1 and F2 mostly have the key pitch movement anchored on the final word in each phrase, the other two speakers conform to this pattern less often. Figure 24 shows the pitch track for an extract from the recording of M2 in which the final falling pitch is anchored on the penultimate (first) syllable of *sangat* ('very') rather than the final word *kencang* ('powerful'). In fact, in the twelve instances in which a falling tone marks the end of a major phrase in the reading of the NWS passage by M2, the anchor point for the falling pitch is on a non-final word in five instances.

F1 similarly has a few instances of the anchor point occurring on non-final words. In Figure 25, after the initial rise on *namun* ('however'), the peak pitch for the main phrase is on the second syllable of *kencang* [kəntʃɐŋ] ('powerful'), reflecting the lack of prominence on the penultimate syllable of this word because it has /ə/; and the words following *kencang* are on a progressively

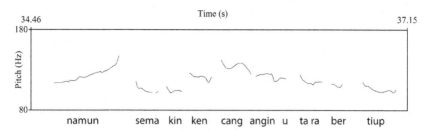

Figure 25 Pitch track of F1 saying *namun semakin kencang angin utara bertiup* ('however, the more powerfully the North Wind blew').

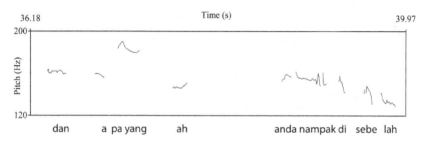

Figure 26 Pitch track of M1 saying *dan apa yang ah (.) anda nampak di sebelah* ('and what do you see at the side') during the male map task.

falling pitch. The pitch contour on the final word, *bertiup* ('to blow'), might be described as level.

In conclusion, on declarative utterances in the NWS passage, non-final phrases tend to have rises and final phrases tend to have falls, and the anchor point for the tone tends to be on the penultimate syllable of the last word (unless it has /ə/). However, this not the only pattern found, and for two of the speakers the anchor point is often found on an earlier word, which is reminiscent of the pattern with fronted topic that was described for Indonesian by Poedjosoedarmo (1986) and was discussed in Section 2.6.

There are no instances of questions in the NWS passage, so, in order to investigate the intonation of Malay questions, we need to consider the map task data. There is a tendency for WH questions (questions that include a question word such as *apa*, 'what', or *di mana*, 'where') to have falling intonation. Figure 26 shows the intonation of an utterance in which M1 produces a WH question with the question word *apa* ('what'). While there is a substantial peak in pitch on the second syllable of *apa*, after that there is a steady fall in pitch throughout the rest of the utterance.

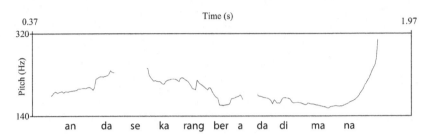

Figure 27 Pitch track of F1 saying *anda sekarang berada di mana* ('where are you now?') during the female map task.

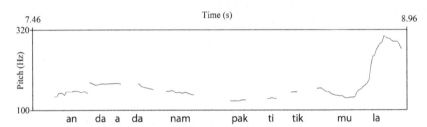

Figure 28 Pitch track of M1 saying *anda ada nampak titik Mula* ('do you see the Start point?') during the male map task.

Not all WH questions have falling intonation. Figure 27 shows F1 producing a WH question with *di mana* ('where') at the start of the recording of the female map task, and there is a clear rise at the end of this utterance.

In total, in the two map task conversations, there are 21 WH questions, most with *apa* ('what') or *di mana* ('where'), and 15 of these WH questions have falling intonation while six have rising intonation.

For YN questions (polar questions that seek a 'yes' or 'no' response), nearly all instances have rising intonation. Figure 28 shows an instance of M1 producing a YN question at the end of the first turn in the male map task conversation.

However, there is a problem here. Unlike in English, in which most YN interrogatives are usually marked syntactically by subject-auxiliary inversion, in Malay most YN questions are not marked syntactically. While there exists a *kah* question particle, its use is quite rare, and most YN questions are simply indicated by means of intonation; so it is circular to note that YN questions are signalled by means of rising intonation and then to conclude that most YN questions have rising intonation. Figure 29 shows an instance in which M1 finishes his turn with a phrase with final rising pitch rather similar to that in Figure 28, but in this case it is not classified as a YN question because it does not appear to function as one. Instead,

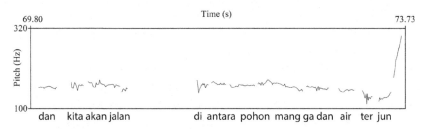

Figure 29 Pitch track of M1 saying *dan kita akan jalan di antara Pohon Mangga dan Air Terjun* ('and we will walk between the Mango Tree and the Waterfall') during the male map task.

the rising phrase-final intonation seems to carry an indication that more is to follow, or perhaps it is encouraging some kind of feedback. Indeed, in this case, M2 responds with *hm-mm*, as a positive backchannel.

Clearly, reliable identification of YN questions is problematic. However, an attempt was made to identify all YN questions based on their function in the conversation. Of the 15 YN questions that occurred in the two map-task conversations, 13 have rising pitch while just two have falling pitch.

This description of the intonation of Malay is preliminary, based on the speech of just four speakers and providing a minimal analysis of some of the pitch patterns that occur. Substantial further research is needed to establish the full inventory of intonational tunes that occur in Malay, how they function in conversational interactions, and how they vary between different speakers and in different varieties of Malay.

6 Future Research

Further investigation into suprasegmental aspects of speech, particularly intonation, would be valuable for all varieties of Malay. Little detailed research has been conducted on the intonation of Malay, to identify the full inventory of tones, determine their patterns of usage, and determine how different speakers produce them in various contexts and in a range of different varieties of Malay. In recent years, the ToBI (Tones and Break Indices) model, originally developed by Pierrehumbert (1980) and elaborated by Ladd (2008), has been adopted to describe the intonation of many different languages using an inventory of high and low tones aligned with accented syllables and tone unit boundaries, but little work has been done using this framework for the description of Malay. This is an area of research that would benefit from detailed investigation, both to provide a full account of the intonation of a range of varieties of Malay and also to facilitate its comparison with the intonation of other languages. Indeed, detailed analysis of how and why the pronunciation of varieties of Malay differs should be a highly productive focus of future research.

The issue of word stress also remains unresolved: while it has been convincingly argued that Malay does not have lexical stress in the same way that English or Dutch do (Maskikit-Essed & Gussenhoven, 2008), some alternative system of prominence is evident, and it might be described as involving the anchoring of H(igh) and L(ow) tones that are fundamental in the ToBI model, so future research might focus on how these tones are aligned with the speech signal, and also how speakers of Malay perceive prominence in their language.

While the analysis of rhythm presented here is consistent with the results of Deterding (2011) in confirming that Malay is more syllable-timed than British English, the study of rhythm would benefit from additional attention, both to investigate how the rhythm of different varieties of Malay depends on the speaker and the context, and also to consider how the rhythm of Malay should be measured. While the nPVI reflects variation along the syllable/stress-timed continuum reasonably well, a comparison of the duration of consecutive vowels does not capture the full essence of rhythm. Nolan and Asu (2009) point out that the nPVI measurements do not have to involve vowel duration, as any consecutive measurements could be used for the calculation, and Fuchs (2016) has shown that some combination of duration and amplitude works better than just vowel duration.

Issues regarding the calculation of the nPVI based on vowel duration in Malay can be illustrated using the single word *pengembara* ('traveller'). In the four syllables of this word, there are two tokens of /ə/, both of which may be very brief, followed by two tokens of /a/, both of which are likely to be much longer, so the nPVI measurements suggest that there are two short syllables followed by two long ones; but this does not reflect the true rhythmic nature of this word that may have four evenly timed syllables [pəŋ.əm.ba.ra], with much of the duration of the first two syllables being in the nasal coda rather than the vowel. One possibility would be to base the measurements on the duration of the whole syllable or maybe on the rhyme (the vowel plus any coda). But determining the location of the end of a syllable is sometimes not straightforward; for example, one must consider the possibility of ambisyllabicity, where a single consonant belongs in two syllables. These issues and others related to the measurement of rhythm might be investigated further with regard to determining the rhythm of Malay.

The analysis conducted here has considered syllable reduction in Standard Malay, particularly the omission of /ə/ after /s/; additional work could study the words in which this tends to occur, and the environments which favour deletion or retention of this vowel. Further research might also focus on other processes occurring in conversational speech, including the omission of syllables and the kinds of assimilation that occur. Indeed, little work has been done on the detailed analysis of the phonetic patterns of conversational Malay.

The consonant of Malay that has the greatest variation is probably /r/, which may typically be realized as a trill, a tap or an approximant, and sometimes as a fricative, or it may be omitted. Although the main variant that occurs in different varieties of Malay has been described by Asmah (1991, pp. 11–12), little is known about how these variant realizations of /r/ depend on the background of the individual speaker, the formality of the speech event, and the phonological context. The study of /r/ in English has offered substantial insights into the speech of people in New York (Labov, 1972) as well as pronunciation in Singapore (Tan, 2012), and the use of non-prevocalic /r/ in English has been shown to have undergone a substantial shift in the speech of young people in Brunei in recent years (Nur Raihan, 2017). The study of variation of the realization of /r/ in Malay offers similar fruitful avenues for research.

The status of various sounds in the inventory of phonemes should be investigated further, particularly the status of the glottal stop and whether it should be listed as a phoneme of Malay. The status of the other marginal consonants /f, v, z, ʃ, x/ would also benefit from additional research, to see if the increasing adoption of loan words in Malay, especially from Arabic and English, is resulting in these sounds becoming more accepted as mainstream consonants in Malay. The classification of the two affricates as plosives with noisy release should also be considered further, as well as the status of diphthongs in Malay.

A detailed study of how the pronunciation of Indonesian differs from Standard Malay, why such differences have arisen, and whether the varieties are now diverging or converging would be valuable.

Issues have been raised about the phonemic analysis of each of the regional dialects of Malay that have been briefly discussed here: How should the nasalised final vowels of Kelantan Malay be analyzed phonologically? Does Brunei Malay have more than three word-final diphthongs, and if it does, how should they be represented phonemically? And how should the long vowels of Kedayan that arise from the absence of final /r/ be treated? Many such phonological issues arise from the detailed analysis of varieties of Malay. Indeed, study of the huge range of dialects of Malay would benefit from extensive further research to establish which varieties are spoken by different people in a range of contexts in Malaysia, Indonesia, Brunei, Singapore, and elsewhere. Indeed, the study of the phonetics of Malay is in its infancy, and there are a huge range of topics for additional research that might be pursued.

Appendix 1 The NWS Passage

In the phonetic transcription of the North Wind and the Sun (NWS) passage by the four consultants, the major pitch movements, particularly at the end of each phrase, are shown with ↗ and ↘.

F1

F1 is 63 years old. She speaks Brunei Malay at home, but she uses Standard Malay with students and conversationally with colleagues. She lived for ten years in Malaysia. F1 read the passage in 69 seconds, a speaking rate of 5.10 syllables per second. This is a phonetic transcription of her reading of the passage:

1 kətike eŋɪn uteɾɐ den meteheɾi sədeŋ bətəŋker mənənai siɐjpɐ jeŋ

2 ləbɪh kwet˼ ↗ | səɔɾeŋ pəŋəmbeɾɐ bərembʊt˼ peɾeŋ ↗ | jeŋ məmɐkaɪ ʤubɐh

3 bəɾwɐɾnɐ meɾɐh ↗ | bərʤɐlɐn məlɐluʷi təmpɐt˼ təsəbʊt˼ ↘ || kəduʷɐduʷɐ

4 bəɾstuʤu ↗ | behɐwɐ siɐpɐ ↗ jeŋ bɔle mənəbɐp˼ken ↗ pəŋəmbeɾɐ itu

5 mənəŋɐlken ʤubɐhɲɐ ↗ || iɐ ɐken diʔeŋɐp˼ ləbɪh kwet˼ ↘ || eŋɪn uteɾɐ
   dəŋɐn

6 sɔmbɔŋ ↗ mənɐteken → | iɐ ↗ jeŋ pɐlɪŋ kwet˼ ↘ di ʔɐnteɾɐ məɾekɐ || lɐlu
   eŋɪn uteɾɐ

7 pʊn ↗ məŋhəmbʊsken ↗ ʔeŋɪn dɪŋɪn jeŋ sɐŋɐt˼ kəɲʧeŋ ↘ || nɐmʊn ↗ |
   səmɐkɪn

8 kəɲʧeŋ ↗ ʔeŋɪn uteɾɐ bəɹtjʊp˼ → | səmɐkɪn eɾɐt˼ ↘ pulɐ pəŋəmbeɾɐ
   təsəbʊt˼ ↗

9 məmbɐlʊt˼ tubuɲɐ dəŋɐn ʤubɐh ↘ || səhɪŋɡɐ ɐhɪɹɲɐ? ↗ eŋɪn uteɾɐ pʊn ↗

10 mənɐlɐh ↘ || kini ↗ tibɐ giliɾɐn meteheɾi mənʊ ndʒʊken helɐhɲɐ ↘ || dəŋɐn
   səɡəɹɐ ↗ |

11 meteheɾi ↗ məmɐɲʧɐɹken sinɐɹɲɐ jeŋ təɹɪ ↘ || ɔle səbɐp˼ kəpɐnɐsɐn ↗ |

12 pəŋəmbeɾɐ təsəbʊt˼ ↗ mənəŋɐlken ↘ ʤubɐhɲɐ → || kəmudien bəɾehɐt˼
   ↗ | lɐlu tətiduɾ↘

13 lene →| kətike bəɹsɐndɐɹ di səbɐtɐŋ pɔkɔʔ rendɐŋ ↗ | jeŋ ↗ bədɐkɐtɐn ↘
   dəŋɐnɲɐ → ||

14 welɐupʊn kəʧɐwɐ ʔɐken kəkɐlɐhɐnɲɐ ↗ | eŋɪn uteɾɐ ↗ təpɐʔsɐ mənɐkwi

15 behɐwɐ || meteheɾi ↗ memɐŋ ləbɪh kwet˼ ↘ dɐɾipɐdɐɲɐ →

F2

F2 is 37 years old. She uses English and both Brunei Malay and Standard Malay at home. She also uses Standard Malay in formal situations. She lived in the United

Kingdom for five years. In the past, she has worked as a part-time newsreader for the national broadcasting company, Radio Television Brunei (RTB), and as a result, she may have some features of formal 'newsreader speech' (Poedjosoedarmo, 1996). F2 was also the informant who read an earlier version of the NWS passage that was described in Clynes and Deterding (2011). F2 read the passage in 74 seconds, representing a speaking rate of 4.76 syllables per second, which is a little more slowly than the other three, perhaps reflecting her experience as a newsreader.

1 kətikɐ ɐɲɪn utɐɾɐ dɛn mɛtɛhɛɾi sədɛŋ bərtəŋkɛr ↗ | mənəne?i siɐjpɐ jɛŋ

2 ləbɪh kʰwɐtˋ ↗ | sə?ɔɾɛŋ ↗ pəŋəmbɛɾɐ ↗ bərɛmbʊtˋ peɾɐŋ ↗ | jɛŋ məmɐkaɪ dʒubɛh ↗

3 bərwɛrnɐ mɛɾɐh ↗ | bərdʒɛlɛn ↗ məlɐluʷi təmpɐtˋ tərsəbʊtˋ ↘ || kəduʷɐduʷɐ ↗

4 bərstudʒu ↘ || bɛhɐwɐ siɐpɐ ↗ jɛŋ bɔlɛh mənəbɐpkɛn ↗ pəŋəmbɛɾɐ itu

5 mənɛŋɡɛlkɛn ↗ dʒubɛhɲɐ ↗ || iɐ ?ɛkɛn di?ɛŋɡɛpˋ ləbɪh ↘ kwɐtˋ || ɐɲɪn utɐɾɐ dəŋɛn

6 sɔmbɔŋ ↘ | mənɛtɛkɛn iɐ jɛŋ pɛlɪŋ ↗ kwɐtˋ ↘ di ?ɛntɛɾɐ mɪɛkɐ ↘ || lɛlu ↗ ɐɲɪn utɐɾɐ

7 pʊn ↗ mənhəmbʊskɛn ↗ ?ɐɲɪn diɲɪn jɛŋ sɐɲɛtˋ kəɲtʃɛŋ ↘ || nɛmʊn ↗ smɐkɪn

8 kəɲtʃɛŋ ↘ ?ɐɲɪn utɐɾɐ bərtiʲʊpˋ ↗ || smɐkɪn ɛɾɐtˋ ↘ pulɐ ↗ || pəŋəmbɛɾɐ tərsəbʊtˋ ↗ |

9 məmbɐlʊtˋ tubuhɲɐ dəŋɛn dʒubɛh ↘ || səhɪŋɡɐ ?ɛxɪɾɲɐ → | ɐɲɪn utɐɾɐ pʊn

10 mənɐlɛh ↘ || kʰini ↗ tibɐ giliɾɛn mɛtɛhɛɾi ↗ mənʊndʒʊkɛn hɛlɐhɲɐ ↘ || dəŋɛn səɡɾɐ → |

11 mɛtɛhɛɾi ↗ məmɐɲtʃɐɪkɛn ↗ sinɐɪɲɐ jɛŋ tərɪkˋ ↘ || ɔlɛh səbɐp kəpɛnɛsɛn ↗ |

12 pəŋəmbɛɾɐ təsəbʊtˋ ↗ mənɛŋɡɛlkɛn dʒubɛhɲɐ ↘ || kəmudiɛn brɛhɐtˋ ↗ | lɛlu tərtidur

13 lɛnɐ →| kətikɐ bəɪsɛndɛɪ di səbɐtɛŋ ↗ pɔkɔ? rɛndɛŋ ↗ | jɛŋ ↗ bərdəkɛtɛn ↘ dəŋɛnɲɐ ||

14 wɛlɐupʊn kətʃɛwɐ ↗ ?ɛkɛn kəkɛlɐhɛnɲɐ ↗ || ɐɲɪn utɐɾɐ ↗ tərpɐ?sɐ mənɐkwi → ||

15 bɛhɐwɐ mɛtɛhɛɾi mɛmɐŋ ↗ ləbɪh kwɐtˋ ↘ dɐɾipɐdɐɲɐ →

M1

M1 is 33 years old. He speaks Brunei Malay and English at home, and he can also speak Dusun. He uses Standard Malay with colleagues and students, in interviews, in meetings, and in formal situations, especially with the older generation of Malay scholars. He has lived abroad for three years in the United Kingdom. He read the passage in 69 seconds, representing a speaking rate of 5.10 syllables per second.

1 kətike ɐŋɪn uteɾɐ dɛn metehɛɾi sədeŋ bəɹtəŋkeɾ ↗ | məŋənɐʔi siɐpɐ jeŋ

2 ləbih kwɐt˺ ↗ | səɔɾɐŋ pəŋəmbɐɾɐ bəɾembʊt˺ peɾɐŋ ↗ | jeŋ məmɛkaɪ dʒubɐh

3 bəɾwɛɹne meɾɐh ↗ | bədʒelen məlɐluʷi tɐmpɐt˺ təsəbʊt˺ ↘ || kəduʷeduʷɐɹɐ

4 bəstudʒu ↘ | behɐwɐ siɐpɐ jeŋ bɔleh ↗ mənəbɐp˺ken ↗ pəŋəmbɐɾɐ itu

5 mənɐŋɡelken dʒubɐhɲɐ ↗ | iʲɐ ɐken diʔɐŋɡɐp˺ ləbɪh kwɐt˺ ↘ || ɐŋɪn uteɾɐ ↗ dəŋɐn

6 sɔmbɔŋ ↗ məŋɐteken iʲɐ ↗ jeŋ pelɪŋ kwɐt˺ di ʔɐntɐɾɐ məɾekɐ ↘ || lɐlu ↗ | ɐŋɪn uteɾɐ ↗

7 pʊn mənhəmbʊsken ↗ ʔɐŋɪn diŋɪn jeŋ sɐŋɐt˺ kəɲtʃeŋ ↘ || nemʊn ↗ | səmɐkɪn

8 kəɲtʃeŋ ↘ ʔɐŋɪn uteɾɐ bəɹtiʲʊp˺ ↗ | səmɐkɪn ɐɾɐt˺ pulɐ pəŋəmbɐɾɐ təsəbʊt˺ ↗

9 məmbɐlʊt˺ tubuɲɐ ↗ dəŋɐn dʒubɐh ↘ || səhɪŋɡɐ ʔɐhɪɹɲɐʔ ↗ ɐŋɪn uteɾɐ pʊn

10 məŋɐlɐh ↘ || kini ↗ tibɐ ɡiliɾɐn metehɛɾi mənʊndʒʊken helɐhɲɐ ↘ || dəŋɐn səɡəɾɐ ↗ |

11 metehɛɾi ↗ məmɐɲtʃɐɹken sineɹɲɐ ↗ jeŋ təɾi? ↘ || ɔleh səbɐp˺ kəpɐnɐsen ↗ |

12 pəŋəmbɐɾɐ təsəbʊt˺ mənɐŋɡelken dʒubɐhɲɐ ↗ | kəmudien bəɾehet˺ ↗ | lɐlu tətiduɹ

13 lenɐ ↘ | kətikɐ bəɹsendeɹ di səbɐteŋ pɔkɔʔ rendeŋ ↗ | jeŋ ↗ bədəketen dəŋɐnɲɐ ↘ ||

14 welɐupʊn kətʃewɐ ↘ ʔɐken kəkɐlehɐnɲɐ ↗ | ʔɐŋɪn uteɾɐ ↗ təpɐʔsɐ məŋɐkwi ↘ |

15 behɐwɐ metehɛɾi ↗ memɐŋ ləbɪ kwɐt˺ dɐɾipɐdɐɲɐ ↘

M2

M2 is 36 years old. He speaks Brunei Malay at home, and he also speaks Tutong and English. He uses Standard Malay with students in the classroom. He has spent four years abroad in the United Kingdom and Germany. M2 read the passage in 68 seconds, a speaking rate of 5.18 syllables per second, which is almost the same as that of F1 and also M1.

1 kətikɐ ʔɐŋɪn uteɾɐ ↗ dɛn metehɛɾi sədeŋ bəɹtəŋker ↘ | məŋənɐʔi sjɐpɐ jeŋ

2 ləbɪh kwɐt˺ ↗ | sɐʔɔɾɐŋ pəŋəmbɐɾɐ bəɾembʊt˺ peɾɐŋ → | jeŋ məmɛkaɪ dʒubɐh ↗

3 bərwɛrnɛ mɛrɛh ↗ | bədʒɛlɛn ↘ mələluʷi təmpɛtˈ ↘ təsəbʊtˈ ‖
kəduʷɛduʷɐɲɐ

4 bəstudʒu ↘ | bɛhɛwɛ siɛpɛ jɛŋ bɔlɛh ↗ məɲəbɛpkɛn ↗ pəŋəmbɛrɛ itu

5 mənɛŋgɛlkɛn dʒubɛhɲɐ ↗ | iʲɛ ʔɛkɛn diʔɛŋgɛpˈ ləbɪ ↘ kwɛtˈ ‖ ɐɲɪn utɛrɛ ↗
dəŋɛn

6 sɔmbɔŋ ↗ məŋɛtɛkɛn → iʲɛ ↗ jɛŋ pɛlɪŋ kwɛtˈ ↘ di ʔɛntɛrɛ mərɛkɛ ‖ lɛlu
↗ | ɐɲɪn utɛrɛ ↗

7 pʊn məɲhəmbʊskɛn ↗ ʔɐɲɪn diɲɪn ↘ jɛŋ sɐɲɛtˈ ↘ kəɲʧɛŋ ‖ nɛmʊn ↗ |
smɛkɪn

8 kəɲʧɛŋ ↗ ʔɐɲɪn utɛrɛ bəɹtjʊpˈ ↘ | smɛkɪn ɛrɛtˈ pulɛ → pəŋəmbɛrɛ təsəbʊtˈ
↗

9 məmbɛdʊtˈ tubuɲɐ dəŋɛn dʒubɛh ↗ ‖ səhɪŋgɛ ɛxɪɲɐ? ↗ ɐɲɪn utɛrɛ pʊn ↗

10 məŋɛlɛh ↘ ‖ kini ↗ tibɛ giliɾɛn mɛtɛhɛɾi ↘ mənʊʒʊkɛn hɛlɐhɲɐ ↘ ‖
dəŋɛn səgərɛ ↗ |

11 mɛtɛhɛɾi məməɲʧɛɹkɛn sinɛrɲɐ ↗ jɛŋ tərɪ? ↘ ‖ ɔlɛ səbɛpˈ kəpɛnɛsɛn ↗ |

12 pəŋəmbɛrɛ tərsəbʊtˈ ↗ mənɛŋgɛlkɛn dʒubɛhɲɐ ↗ | kəmudiɛn bərɛhɛtˈ ↗ |
lɛlu tərtiduɾ

13 lɛnɛ ↘ | kətikɛ bərsɛndɛɾ ↗ di səbɛtɛŋ ↗ pɔkɔ? rɛndɛŋ ↗ | jɛŋ ↗
bərdəkɛtɛn dəŋɛnɲɐ ↘ ‖

14 wɛlɛupʊn ↗ kəʧɛwɛ ↘ ʔɛkɛn kəkɛlɛhɐnɲɐ ↗ | ɐɲɪn utɛrɛ ↗ tərpɛkʔsɛ
↗ məŋɛkwi

15 bɛhɛwɛ → | mɛtɛhɛɾi mɛmɛŋ ləbɪh kwɛtˈ ↘ dɛɾipɛdɐɲɐ

Appendix 2 The Map Task

In the transcripts of the two map task recordings, the number on the left of the start of each turn shows the time in seconds from the beginning of the recording. Pauses are shown with the time in seconds in brackets, for example, (1.2); pauses shorter than 0.5 seconds are shown as (.). Overlaps are shown with <num> </num>. Loud syllables are shown in upper case.

Female Map Task

00 F1 anda sekarang berada di mana

02 F2 saya berada di atas pohon mangga

04 F1 okay hh <low> di atas </low> pohon mangga ataupun di sekitar (.) pohon mangga

09 F2 jika dilihat dari segi ah: (0.5) dimensi dua 'd' saya berada di atas pohon mangga

15 F1 okay baiklah oh terpaksa turun dulu (0.9) untuk menuju ke: (0.5) arah yang dituju (0.7) okay (1.5) <quiet> ah: </quiet> (0.6) baiklah (.) seterusnya untuk (.) menuju ke: kawasan ladang tani (0.6) pertama setelah awda turun dari pokok mangga (0.6) awda terus perjalanan (0.6) ah: (1.7) di s- di sebelah: (0.9) kanan awda (.) ada air terjun (2.3) ah teruskan lagi (0.6) perjalanan (.) dan (0.8) di sebelah kanan juga ada padang rumput berpagar (1.7)

51 F2 jadi saya perlu: (.) ah mel- me: melimpasi air terjun dan hutan menuju ke padang rumput berpagar

59 F1 ah: (0.9) hutan saya tidak (.) sini tidak ada hutan tetapi di: (0.8) di: di sini ada padang rumput berpagar

67 F2 jadi terus saja dari air terjun ke padang rumput berpagar

70 F1 ya dan teruskan lagi di sebelah kiri awda ada pondok terbiar (1.9) <quiet> ah </quiet> (0.5) teruskan lagi perjalanan (.) sehingga awda (.) di sebelah (.) kiri awda ada padang rumput berpagar lagi (1.3)

84 F2 adakah saya perlu: me:lewati mercu tanda

88 F1 <1> mercu </1>

88 F2 <1> atau adakah </1> padang rumput berpagar berada (.) di antara (.) jambatan baharu dan mercu tanda

94 F1 ah: (.) <2> mercu </2>

95 F2 di manakah <2> letaknya </2> padang rumput berpagar

97   F1   mercu ta- ah padang rumput berpagar berada di sebelah kiri sebelum jambatan: (.) jambatan baharu

103   F2   sebelum jambatan baharu

104   F1   ya

104   F2   maknanya di bawah jambatan baharu

106   F1   mm: di bawah di se- (.) sebelum

120   F2   sebelum

111   F1   <3> ya </3>

111   F2   <3> jambatan </3> baharu

112   F1   ya (.) sebelum jambatan baharu

114   F2   maknanya di sebelah kiri pondok terbiar

118   F1   ya e- (0.9) sebelah bukan sebelah ki- a baratnya berhampiran dengan pondok terbiar (.) sebelah kiri (1.8) ah: seterusnya awda: (.) anda: (.) ah menyeberangi jambatan baharu

132   F2   mm

133   F1   dan melempasi: (.) tasik barat di sebelah kiri (1.7)

138   F2   kenapa saya perlu melalui (.) ke sebelah kiri

141   F1   ah:: (1.2) tidak perlu sebelah kiri ↓ tetapi tasik (0.6) tasik barat itu berada di sebelah kiri

147   F2   <4> ah </4>

147   F1   dan <4> seterusnya </4> awda akan membelok ke:

149   F2   jadi tasik barat saya perlu melimpasi jamba- saya perlu melalui jambatan <5> baha ru </5>

153   F1   <5> melalui </5> jambatan

155   F2   <6> dan </6>

155   F1   <6> dan </6> tasik barat

156   F2   dan tasik barat akan berada di sebelah

158   F1   kiri

159   F2   kiri saya

160   F1   ah dan seterusnya ba- (0.5) awda menuju ke: mercu tanda (3.1)

166   F2   ada berapa mercu tanda pada um

168   F1   sat- (.) hanya <7> satu mercu </7>

169   F2   <7> pada kertas anda </7>

170   F1   ha:nya: ada satu mercu tanda

172   F2   jadi saya perlu turun semula ke mercu tanda

174   F1   ya mercu tanda (3.6) dan meneruskan perjalanan (0.6) ah: (.) melalui bukit (.) yang berada di sebelah (0.6) kanan anda (2.7)

188   F2   ada ah: di manakah lokasi bukit

191   F1   bukit ber- berada di lokasi: (.) di sebelah kanan: (1.6) <8> jalan mercu tanda </8>

197 F2 <8> kanan mercu tanda </8>

198 F1 ya di sebelah kanan

199 F2 di bawah maknanya di bawah padang bola (0.9)

202 F1 ah sa: (.) tidak ada padang bola di sini (.) cuma yang ada tasik timur (0.9)

206 F2 <quiet> baik </quiet> (1.7) jadi mercu tanda: (0.6) dan: melimpasi: <9> bukit </9>

212 F1 <9> bukit </9>

213 F2 menuju ke tasik timur

214 F1 yes (.) ya

Male Map Task

00 M1 baik ah kita akan mulakan dengan ah: (0.7) bermula dari titik mula dahulu (.) ah: (0.9) anda ada nampak titik mula

09 M2 ya

09 M1 ah (0.7) baiklah ah: (.) dep- (.) berdepanan dengan titik mula (.) ah: apa yang ah: anda nampak (1.4)

17 M2 ada pondok (.) terbiar

19 M1 ah:

19 M2 di sebelah: (.) kanan

21 M1 ah berdepanan dengan (.) titik mula (2.0)

25 M2 s:epohon mangga

27 M1 ah sepohon mangga

28 M2 hm-hm

28 M1 ah: (.) baik ah: kita akan jalan MENGelilingi ah pohon mangga tersebut

33 M2 hm

34 M1 ah: mengelilingi dahulu (0.5) da:n apa yang ah (0.7) anda nampak di sebelah <creak> ah: </creak> (0.5) ki- kanan (0.9)

43 M2 ah AIR terjun

44 M1 di sebelah kanan: (.) daripada pohon mangga (1.1)

48 M2 satu air terjun

49 M1 air terjun hh ah: (.) jadinya kita akan jalan ah: (.) berdekatan dengan pohon mangga d- ah depan pohon mangga ta- ah ada apa-apakah (0.9)

58 M2 ada se:buah rumah panjang

59 M1 ah sebuah rumah panjang

61 M2 hm-hm

62	M1	ah baik ah saya tiada s- rumah panjang sana hh ah kita jala- akan jalan terus: (.) melintasi: m- \<creak> ah: \</creak> dan kita akan jalan (0.8) di antara pohon mangga dan air terjun
73	M2	hm-hm (0.7)
75	M1	ah: kita akan jalan (.) ke atas (1.6)
78	M2	hm-hm
78	M1	ah: (1.6) kita jalan terus (.) ah apa yang ah: (1.1) ah anda nampak di sebelah ah kanan
88	M2	ah: (1.3) satu pondok terbiar
92	M1	s- sebelah kanan ke pondok terbiar
96	M2	hm-hm
96	M1	ah: (0.9) kalau ah anda jalan terus saja daripada air terjun
101	M2	HUtan
102	M1	ah ada ah hutan dah
103	M2	hm-hm
103	M1	baikLAH saya tiada hutan di seba- di sebalah (0.7) ah: di sebalah (.) mana tu
109	M2	sebelah: (.) kanan (.) \<1> air terjun \</1>
111	M1	\<1> sebelah kanan \</1> (0.5) baik ah kita akan jalan terus
114	M2	hm-hm
114	M1	jadinya ah: jalan terus ah ke depan
117	M2	mm
118	M1	apa yang (.) anda nampak
121	M2	padang rumput berpagar
123	M1	baiklah ah: (.) padang rumput berpagar (.) ah: (.) jadi kita akan ah: (0.7) jalan ke atas lagi
130	M2	hm-hm
130	M1	kita jalan-jalan terus dan: ah apa yang (.) anda nampak seterusnya
136	M2	pondok terbiar
137	M1	baik (.) baiklah pondok terbiar ah: (1.1) ah: (.) boleh terangkan mengenai pondok terbiar tersebut (1.6)
146	M2	se- se:buah pondok terbiar bersaiz kecil
149	M1	hm-hm
150	M2	mm: di sebelah hadapannya ada satu pintu dan satu tingkap kecil
154	M1	hm-hm (0.6) jadinya k- ah: di sebalah ah di sebelah (.) m- mana tadi
160	M2	sebelah: atas
161	M1	ah \<2> s- s- \</2>
161	M2	padang \<2> rumput \</2> berpagar
163	M1	sebelah (0.5) ad- (0.8) anda di mana ketika ini
167	M2	pondok terbiar

168 M1 ah dekat po- pondok terbiar ya (0.5) okay kita jalan terus ke atas lagi (0.7) kita jalan terus ke atas dan kita ah: (1.1) pusing ke: sebelah kiri (1.1)

179 M2 hm-hm

179 M1 dan jalan ter- jalan terus (.) dan apa yang ah: anda nampak di hadapan (.) anda sekarang

184 M2 jambatan baharu (0.7)

186 M1 ah: (0.5) jambatan baharu

188 M2 mm (0.8)

189 M1 dekat dengan jambatan baharu tadi ap- apa yang ada ah: (0.7) anda a: da nampak

194 M2 sebelum jambatan baharu pondok terbiar

198 M1 hm-hm

197 M2 dan (:) bila ke sebelah kiri ada jambatan baharu

199 M1 hm-hm

200 M2 dan selepas jambatan baharu ada: satu TASIK barat

203 M1 okay ah ini kita akan ah: merentasi: jambatan baharu tadi kan

208 M2 hm-hm

208 M1 kita akan jalan terus (0.6) ah: (.) dan s- (.) kini apa yang ada dekat ah yang (.) anda nampak

215 M2 ah: selepas tasik barat ada LADANG tani

219 M1 ladang-ladang tani baiklah ah: (.) ada (.) ah: (.) ada nampak <creak> ah: </creak> (0.4) mercu tanda di sana (0.7)

227 M2 mercu tanda di sebelah kanan: (.) atas pondok terbiar

231 M1 okay ah kita akan (.) ah pusing lagi

233 M2 hm-hm

234 M1 daripada (0.5) tadi tasik barat kan

236 M2 hm-hm

236 M1 kita akan: ah pusing lagi ke: menuju ke: ah: (0.6) arah tersebut

241 M2 hm-hm

241 M1 ke mercu tanda (0.9) dan: (0.6) kita mengelilingi (.) mercu tanda (0.9) dan naik ke atas

250 M2 hm-hm

250 M1 apa yang ah: anda nampak (0.8) <3> sekarang </3>

252 M2 <3> padang bola </3>

253 M1 padang bola

254 M2 hm-hm

255 M1 okay ah s- (.) okay saya (.) saya tidak ada (.) padang bola di sini hh jadinya ah: kita akan ah (0.6) LINtasi (0.5) padang bola (.) dan naik ke atas (0.9) ah: apa yang ah anda nampak sekarang

268 M2   s:ebu- satu tasik timur

270 M1   ah satu: sebuah tasik timur

272 M2   hm-hm

273 M1   dan kita akan: terus (.) menuju ke: ah: sebelah kiri (1.1) dan sebelah
          kiri apa yang anda nampak (.) <quiet> sekarang </quiet>

282 M2   tamat

283 M1   ah tamat dan kita akan menamatkan ah perjalanan di sana

288 M2   hm-hm

References

Abdullah Hassan. (2005). *Linguistik am* [*General linguistics*] (2nd ed.). PTS Professional Sdn. Bhd.

Abdul Hamid Mahmood & Nurfarah Loo Abdullah. (2013). *Linguistik fonetik dan fonologi Bahasa Melayu* [*The phonetics and phonology of Malay linguistics*]. Syarikat Pencetakan Muncul Sistem Sdn Bhd.

Abercrombie, D. (1967). *Elements of general phonetics*. Edinburgh University Press.

Abramson, A. S. (2003). Acoustic cues to word-initial stop length in Pattani Malay. *Proceedings of the 15th International Congress of Phonetic Sciences* (pp. 387–90). 3–9 August, 2003, Barcelona.

Adelaar, K. A. (1992). *Proto Malayic: The reconstruction of its phonology and parts of its lexicon and morphology*. Pacific Linguistics.

Adelaar, K. A. (2005). The Austronesian languages of South East Asia and Madagascar: A historical perspective. In K. A. Adelaar & N. Himmelmann (Eds.), *The Austronesian languages of Asia and Madagascar* (pp. 1–41). Routledge.

Andaya, L. Y. (2001). The search for the 'origins' of Melayu. *Journal of Southeast Asian Studies, 32*(3), 315–30.

Anderson, A. H., Bader, M., Bard, E. G. et al. (1991). The HCRC map task corpus. *Language and Speech, 34*(4), 351–66.

Asmah Haji Omar. (1967). Towards the unification of Bahasa Melayu and Bahasa Indonesia: An account of efforts to standardize the spelling system of Malay in Malaysia and Indonesia. *Tenggara, 1*(1). [Reprinted in Asmah Haji Omar (Ed.), (1975). *Essays on Malay linguistics* (pp. 45–49). Dewan Bahasa dan Pustaka.]

Asmah Haji Omar. (1971). Standard language and the standardization of Malay. *Anthropological Linguistics*, February 1971. [Reprinted in Asmah Haji Omar (Ed.), (1975). *Essays on Malay linguistics* (pp. 50–70). Dewan Bahasa dan Pustaka.]

Asmah Haji Omar. (1985). *Susur galur Bahasa Melayu* [*The genealogy of Malay*]. Dewan Bahasa dan Pustaka.

Asmah Haji Omar. (1991). *The phonological diversity of the Malay dialects* (2nd ed.). Dewan Bahasa dan Pustaka.

Asmah Haji Omar. (2008). *Ensiklopedia Bahasa Melayu* [*Encyclopedia of the Malay language*]. Dewan Bahasa dan Pustaka.

Berkovitz, R. (1984). Duration and fundamental frequency in sentence-final intonation. *Journal of Phonetics, 12,* 255–65.

Boersma, P., & Weenink, D. (2020). *Praat: Doing phonetics by computer* (Version 6.1.15). Accessed at www.fon.hum.uva.nl/praat

Clynes, A. (1997). On the Proto-Austronesian 'diphthongs'. *Oceanic Linguistics, 36,* 347–62.

Clynes, A. (2014). Brunei Malay: An overview. In P. Sercombe, M. Boutin & A. Clynes (Eds.), *Advances in research on linguistic and cultural practices in Borneo* (pp. 153–200). Borneo Research Council.

Clynes, A., & Deterding, D. (2011). Standard Malay (Brunei). *Journal of the International Phonetic Association, 41*(2), 259–68.

Dauer, R. M. (1983). Stress-timing and syllable-timing reanalyzed. *Journal of Phonetics, 11,* 51–62.

Deterding, D. (2006). The North Wind versus a Wolf: Short texts for the description and measurement of English pronunciation. *Journal of the International Phonetic Association, 36*(2), 187–96.

Deterding, D. (2011). Measurements of the rhythm of Malay. *Proceedings of the 17th International Congress of Phonetic Sciences,* Hong Kong, 17–21 August 2011, pp. 576–9.

Deterding, D. (2012). Issues in the acoustic measurement of rhythm. In J. Romero-Trillo (Ed.), *Pragmatics and prosody in English language teaching* (pp. 9–24). Springer.

Deterding, D., & Ho, H. M. Y. (2021). An overview of the language, literature and culture of Brunei Darussalam. In H. M. Y. Ho & D. Deterding (Eds.), *Engaging modern Brunei: Research on language, literature, and culture.* Springer.

Deterding, D., & Ishamina Athirah. (2017). Brunei Malay. *Journal of the International Phonetic Association, 47*(1), 99–108.

Deterding, D., & Nolan, F. (2007). Aspiration and voicing of Chinese and English plosives. In J. Trouvain & W. J. Barry (Eds.), *Proceedings of the 16th International Congress of Phonetic Sciences, ICPhS XVI* (pp. 385–8), Saarbrücken, 6–10 August 2007.

Dewan Bahasa dan Pustaka (DBP). (2007). *Kamus Bahasa Melayu Brunei* [*Dictionary of Brunei Malay*] (2nd ed.). Dewan Bahasa dan Pustaka.

Dewan Bahasa dan Pustaka (DBP). (2013, 1 October). Taling. *Pusat Rujukan Persuratan Melayu.* Dewan Bahasa dan Pustaka. Accessed at http://prpm .dbp.gov.my/Cari1?keyword=taling&d=175768&

Dewan Bahasa dan Pustaka Brunei (DBPB). (2006). *Kamus Kedayan-Melayu Melayu-Kedayan* [*Dictionary of Kedayan-Malay and Malay-Kedayan*]. Dewan Bahasa dan Pustaka Brunei.

Dewan Bahasa dan Pustaka Brunei (DBPB). (2011). *Daftar leksikal 7 dialek Brunei Darussalam [Lexical list of the 7 dialects of Brunei Darussalam].* Dewan Bahasa dan Pustaka Brunei.

Docherty, G. (1992). *The timing of voicing in British English obstruents.* Foris Publications.

Eades, D., & Hajek, J. (2006). Gayo. *Journal of the International Phonetic Association, 36,* 107–15.

Ebing, E. F., & van Heuvan, V. J. (1997). Some formal and functional aspects of Indonesian intonation. In C. Odé & W. Stokhof (Eds.), *Proceedings of the Seventh International Conference on Austronesian Linguistics,* Leiden, 22–7 August 1994 (pp. 45–61). Rodopi.

Faahirah, R. (2014). The intonation of questions in Brunei. *Southeast Asia: A Multidisciplinary Journal, 14,* 23–8.

Faahirah, R. (2016). Code-switching in Brunei: Evidence from the map task. *South East Asia: A Multidisciplinary Journal, 16,* 65–81.

Faahirah, R., & Deterding, D. (2019). The pronunciation of Kedayan. *South East Asia: A Multidisciplinary Journal, 19,* 78–85.

Farid Onn (1980). *Aspects of Malay phonology and morphology: A generative approach.* Universiti Kebangsaan Malaysia Press.

Fauzi Syamsuar (2018). *Phonological aspects in word formations.* Universitas Ibn Khaldun Bogor.

Ferguson, C. (1959). Diglossia. *Word, 15,* 325–40.

Fuchs, R. (2016). *Speech rhythm in varieties of English: Evidence from educated Indian English and British English.* Springer.

Goedemans, R., & van Zanten, E. (2007). Stress and accent in Indonesian. In V. J. van Heuven & E. van Zanten (Eds.), *Prosody in Indonesian languages.* LOT Occasional Series, *9,* 35–62.

Grabe, E., & Low, E. L. (2002). Durational variability in speech and the rhythm class hypothesis. In C. Gussenhoven, & N. Warner (Eds.), *Laboratory Phonology 7* (pp. 515–46). Mouton de Gruyter.

Gut, U., & Pillai, S. (2014). The question intonation of Malay speakers of English. In E. Delais-Roussarie, M. Avanzi, & S. Herment (Eds.), *Prosody and languages in contact: L2 acquisition, attrition, languages in multilingual situations* (pp. 51–70). Springer.

Hamzah, H., Fletcher, J., & Hajek, J. (2011). Durational correlates of word-initial voiceless geminate stops: The case of Kelantan Malay. In W.-S. Lee & E. Zee (Eds.), *Proceedings of the 17th International Congress of Phonetic Sciences* (pp. 815–18), 17–21 August 2011, Hong Kong.

Hayward, K. (2000). *Experimental phonetics.* Longman.

Hoequist, C. E. (1983). The perceptual center and rhythm categories, *Language and Speech, 26*, 367–76.

Indirawati Zahid & Mardian Shah Omar. (2006). *Fonetik dan fonologi [Phonetics and phonology]*. PTS Professional Sdn. Bhd.

International Phonetic Association (IPA). (1999). *Handbook of the International Phonetic Association*. Cambridge University Press.

Labov, W. (1972). *Sociolinguistic patterns*. University of Pennsylvania Press.

Ladd, D. R. (2008). *Intonational phonology* (2nd ed.). Cambridge University Press.

Ladefoged, P., & Johnson, K. (2011). *A course in phonetics* (6th ed.). Wadsworth Cengage Learning.

Liaw, Y. F. (1999). *Malay grammar made easy: A comprehensive guide*. Times Books International.

Low, E. L., Grabe, E., & Nolan, F. (2000). Quantitative characterizations of speech rhythm: Syllable-timing in Singapore English. *Journal of Phonetics, 29*, 217–30.

Martin, P. (1996). Brunei Malay and Bahasa Melayu: A sociolinguistic perspective. In P. Martin, C. Ożóg, & G. Poedjosoedarmo (Eds.), *Language use and language change in Brunei Darussalam* (pp. 27–36). Ohio University Center for International Studies.

Maskikit-Essed, R., & Gussenhoven, C. (2008). No stress, no pitch accent, no prosodic focus: The case of Ambonese Malay. *Phonology, 33*, 353–89.

McCloy, D. R. (2012). Vowel normalization and plotting with the phonR package. *Technical Reports of the UW Linguistic Phonetics Laboratory #2012–01*.

McLellan, J., Noor Azam Haji-Othman, & Deterding, D. (2016). The language situation in Brunei Darussalam. In Noor Azam Haji-Othman., J. McLellan, & D. Deterding (Eds.), *The use and status of language in Brunei Darussalam: A kingdom of unexpected linguistic diversity* (pp. 9–16). Springer.

Miller, M. (1984). On the perception of rhythm, *Journal of Phonetics, 12*, 75–83.

Mohd Azidan Bin Abdul Jabar. (2004). Gangguan bunyi Melayu dalam sebutan Arab: Satu analisis ringkas [Interference of the sounds of Malay on the pronunciation of Arabic loanwords: A brief analysis]. *Pertanika Journal of Social Sciences & Humanities (JSSH), 12*(2), 101–10.

Nolan, F., & Asu, E. L. (2009). The pairwise variability index and coexisting rhythms in language. *Phonetica, 66*, 64–77.

Nothofer, B. (1991). The languages of Brunei Darussalam. In H. Steinhauer (Ed.), *Papers in Pacific linguistics* (pp. 151–76). Australian National University.

Nur Raihan, M. (2017). Rhoticity in Brunei English: A diachronic approach. *South East Asia: A Multidisciplinary Journal*, *17*, 1–7.

O'Connor, J. D., & Arnold, G. F. (1973). *Intonation of colloquial English: A practical handbook* (2nd ed.). Longman.

Odé, C. (1997). On the perception of prominence in Indonesian: An experiment. In C. Odé & W. Stokhof (Eds.), *Proceedings of the Seventh International Conference on Austronesian Linguistics*, Leiden, 22–27 August 1994 (pp. 150–66). Rodopi.

Pierrehumbert, J. B. (1980). The phonology and phonetics of English intonation. PhD thesis, Massachusetts Institute of Technology. Indiana University Linguistics Club.

Poedjosoedarmo, G. (1986). Subject selection and subject shifting in Indonesian. *NUSA Linguistic Studies of Indonesian and Other Languages in Indonesia*, *25*, 1–18.

Poedjosoedarmo, G. (1996). Variation and change in the sound systems of Brunei dialects of Malay. In P. Martin, C. Ożóg & G. Poedjosoedarmo (Eds.), *Language use and language change in Brunei Darussalam* (pp. 37–42). Ohio University Center for International Studies.

R Core Team (2016). R: A language and environment for statistical computing (Version 3.3.2). R Foundation for Statistical Computing, Vienna, Austria. Accessed at www.R-project.org.

Nur Raihan, M. (2017). Rhoticity in Brunei English: A diachronic approach. *South East Asia: A Multidisciplinary Journal*, *17*, 1–7.

Roach, P. (1982). On the distinction between 'stress-timed' and 'syllable-timed' languages. In D. Crystal (Ed.), *Linguistic Controversies* (pp. 73–9). Edward Arnold.

Ryding, K. C. (2014). *Arabic: A linguistic introduction*. Cambridge University Press.

Sato Hirobumi Rahmat. (2015). *Panduan diftong dan rangkap vokal Bahasa Melayu: Analisis akustik berkomputer* [*A guide to diphthongs and double vowels in Malay: An acoustic analysis*]. Dewan Bahasa dan Pustaka Brunei.

Sneddon, J. (2003). Diglossia in Indonesian. *Bijdragen tot de Taal-, Land- ev Volkenkunde 159*, 519–49.

Soderberg, C. D. (2014a). Cocos Malay. *Journal of the International Phonetic Association*, *44*, 103–7.

Soderberg, C. D. (2014b). Kedayan. *Journal of the International Phonetic Association*, *44*, 201–5.

Soderberg, C. D., & Olson, K. S. (2008). Indonesian. *Journal of the International Phonetic Association*, *38*, 209–13.

Steinhauer, H. (2005). Colonial history and language policy in insular Southeast Asian and Madagascar. In K. Alexander Adelaar & Nikolaus Himmelmann (Eds.), *The Austronesian languages of Asia and Madagascar* (pp. 65–86). Routledge.

Tan, Y. (2012). To r or not to r: Social correlates of /ɹ/ in Singapore English. *International Journal of the Sociology of Language, 218*, 1–24.

Teoh, B. S. (1994). *The sound system of Malay revisited*. Dewan Bahasa dan Pustaka.

Traunmüller, H. (1990). Analytical expressions for the tonotopic sensory scale. *Journal of the Acoustical Society of America, 88*(1), 97–100.

van Heuven, V. J., & Faust, V. (2009). Are Indonesians sensitive to contrastive accentuation below the word level? *Wacana: Jurnal Ilmu Pengetahuan Budaya, 11*(2), 226–40.

van Zanten, E. (1986). Allophonic variation in the production of Indonesian vowels. *Bijdragen tot de Taal-, Land- en Volkenkunde 142*, 427–46.

van Zanten, E., Goedemans, R., & Pacilly, J. (2003). The status of word stress in Indonesian. In J. van de Weijer, V. J. van Heuven, & H. van der Hulst (Eds.), *The phonological spectrum*, vol. 2 (pp. 151–75). John Benjamins.

van Zanten, E., & van Heuven, V. J. (2004). Word stress in Indonesian: Fixed or free? *NUSA, 53*, 1–20.

Wan Aslynn Salwani Wan Ahmad. (2012). Instrumental phonetic study of the rhythm of Malay. Unpublished PhD thesis. Newcastle University.

Wan Aslynn Salwani Wan Ahmad. (2019). Identifying acoustic correlates of stress in Malay words. In Y. N. Thai & J. Setter (Eds.). *Speech research in a Malaysian context* (pp. 53–77). Universiti Putra Malaysia Press.

Wells, J. C. (2008). *Longman pronunciation dictionary* (3rd ed.). Longman.

Wells, J. C. (2006). *English intonation: An introduction*. Cambridge University Press.

Yunus Maris, M. (1980). *The Malay sound system*. Penerbit Fajar Bakti Sdn Bhd.

Zaharani Ahmad. (1993). *Fonologi generatif: Teori dan penerapan* [*Generative phonology: Theory and application*]. Dewan Bahasa dan Pustaka.

Zuraidah Mohd. Don, & Knowles, G. (2006). Prosody and turn-taking in Malay broadcast interviews. *Journal of Pragmatics, 38*, 490–512.

Zuraidah Mohd. Don, Knowles, G., & Yong, J. (2008). How words can be misleading: A study of syllable timing and 'stress' in Malay. *The Linguistics Journal, 3*(2). Accessed at www.linguistics-journal.com/August_2008_zmd .php

Cambridge Elements ⹀

Phonetics

Elements in the Series

The Phonetics of Malay
David Deterding, Ishamina Athirah Gardiner, Najib Noorashid

A full series listing is available at: www.cambridge.org/EIPH

Printed in the United States
by Baker & Taylor Publisher Services